MEXICAN FOLK PLAYS

THE PLAYMAKERS THEATRE

The home of The Carolina Playmakers. The first theatre building in America to be dedicated to the making of its own native drama.

THE CAROLINA PLAYMAKERS SERIES

MEXICAN FOLK PLAYS,

by Josephina Niggli

FOLK PLAYS OF EASTERN CAROLINA

by Bernice Kelly Harris

(*in preparation*)

MEXICAN FOLK PLAYS

BY

JOSEPHINA NIGGLI

EDITED

with an Introduction by

FREDERICK H. KOCH

FOUNDER AND DIRECTOR OF

The Carolina Playmakers

ILLUSTRATED

With Photographs of the Original Productions of the Plays

Chapel Hill

THE UNIVERSITY OF NORTH CAROLINA PRESS

A royalty fee is required for each performance of any of these plays, either by amateurs or by professionals. Special arrangements must be made for radio broadcasting.

No performance of these plays may be given without full acknowledgment to The Carolina Playmakers, Inc., and to The University of North Carolina Press. Acknowledgment should be made to read as follows: "From the MEXICAN FOLK PLAYS, *edited by Frederick H. Koch, Director. Produced by arrangements with The Carolina Playmakers, Inc., and with The University of North Carolina Press."*

The amateur acting rights to these plays are controlled by Samuel French, 25 West 45th Street, New York, N. Y., or 811 West 7th Street, Los Angeles, Calif., to whom application should be made for production.

To My Mother and to Sam Selden
Without Whom These Plays Would
Never Have Been Written

MEXICO, MY BELOVED

Mexico, my beloved,
is not the clashing of cymbals
nor the curving
of vermilion sails
over the heart
of the wind;
it is not
a vivid slash
across the mouth
of the world.

But when the moon touches the silken waves
of the Lerma,
and the carnations
breathe their scents
into the souls of a thousand birds
forcing them to sing
of something
they but dimly understand—
this, my beloved,
is Mexico.

—J. N.

REPRINTED BY PERMISSION FROM *The North American Review*

PLAYMAKER OF MEXICO

"He on whose heart the dust of Mexico has lain will find no rest in any other land," says an old Mexican proverb.

Mexican Folk Plays introduces a new poet in the theatre. Although only twenty-five years of age when these plays were written, Josephina Niggli has shown not a little facility in both the one-act and the full-length form. She understands the lives of her people, their restless history, their legends and the childlike wonder of their folkways. In *Azteca* is the soul of the prehistoric culture of an outlived past; in *Soldadera (Soldier-Woman)*, the heroic struggle of Mexican Valkyries in the Revolution of 1910; in *The Red Velvet Goat, Sunday Costs Five Pesos,* and *Tooth or Shave,* the gay comedy of Mexican village life today.

Josephina Niggli was born in Monterrey, Nuevo Leon, Mexico. From childhood she looked so much like her father that she is still called "Little Niggli" by all his friends. Her mother, a former concert violinist, is well known throughout the Southwest as a teacher of music for children. Her home is an old Mexican estate with a *casa grande* (great house), *La Quinta del Carmen,* "The Garden of Flowers," of many acres and many servants. The favorite in the family is her grandmother, affectionately known to everyone as *La Mamá.* On Sunday evenings an orchestra conducted by the gardener's son-in-law comes to the great house saying, "We have come to serenade *La Mamá.*" Josephina says, "If anyone has plans of doing anything other than listen to the music he may just as well forget about it for the time being."

With the exception of four months spent in the American school in Mexico City, Miss Niggli was taught by her mother until she entered the Main Avenue High School in San Antonio, Texas. From there she went to the Incarnate Word College, where she was much encouraged in her writing by Dr. R. E. Roehl, Head of the English Department.

In the summer of 1935 Miss Niggli came to the University of North Carolina for playwriting. Her decision to come to Chapel Hill was enthusiastically endorsed by Señor Pinza, attaché at the Bolivian embassy in Mexico City, himself a well-known playwright in his own country. During her first year at the University, The Carolina Playmakers produced the plays included in this volume and another short play, *The Cry of Dolores*, about the impassioned leadership of Father Hidalgo in the struggle for independence in 1810. In 1936 she wrote her first full-length play, *Singing Valley*, of the conflict between the old and the new order in Mexico today. In February of the next year The Playmakers produced her second full-length play, *The Fair-God*, of the ill-fated, Utopian dream of the Mexican Empire of Maximilian and Carlota.

Miss Niggli has acting talent too. She appeared in several of the productions of her own plays and directed some of them.

TOOTH OR SHAVE

Tooth or Shave is characteristic of the simple lives of the Mexican village folk. It was produced originally for the Playmakers' Northern tour in November, 1935, and proved such a favorite with the audiences that it was revived for touring purposes the following season.

It is interesting to recall how Miss Niggli's first Mexican folk comedy came to be written: "Anselmo, whose real name is Porfirio, is a barber living in a little town near my own town of Hidalgo. He is the brother of our watchman, and when I was small he used to ride me around on his broad shoulders whenever he came to the house to visit old Nacho. I remember how startled he was when I, with all the dignity of eleven, informed him that the earth moved around the sun. Of all the Mexicans I have ever known, Porfirio, with the mind and heart of a child, is still my favorite.

"The story of the blackmailing scheme grew out of an argument I once heard between Porfirio and Nacho when they were trying to show each other and me how brave they really were. Although now I realize that it was just so much talk, at the time I actually thought that any moment Porfirio was going to kneel down and have his head struck off.

"The story of Mariá's ten pesos, which she was saving for her funeral, is not as absurd as it may seem, as many of the poorer class women in Mexico do just that."

The response to *Tooth or Shave* on tour was well phrased by the reviewer for *The Daily Princetonian* of Princeton University who was impressed by the "simplicity and richness" of The Carolina Playmakers' contribution to a new native drama.

SOLDADERA

Soldadera (*Soldier-Woman*) is a drama of the Agrarian Revolution of 1910 in which the soldier-women are presented for the first time in dramatic form. It portrays with remarkable insight and vividness the effect of the Revolution on the women—"the women who left their homes and dragged along after their men, cooking for them, tending their wounds, guarding their ammunition, fighting when necessary."

To the author the true *soldaderas* were the women for whom there was no blazing patriotic fire. They were "broken shells whose only desire was revenge for all they had suffered during those horror-ridden years before 1910. For them there was no beautiful past, no glorious future. Their only consolation was to weep over the graves of their dead. Unfortunately there are no graves for dead dreams."

Soldadera was produced by The Carolina Playmakers at Chapel Hill on their forty-fourth bill of new plays on February 27, 28 and 29, 1936.

THE RED VELVET GOAT

The Red Velvet Goat is a *saenete*, a Spanish type of drama unknown to the English speaking stage, but widely popular in Mexico. Miss Niggli tells us that the term *saenete* cannot be translated exactly into English, although it is vaguely defined by the dictionary as a kind of farce; that it is simply a picture of what we call the "lower classes" lifted from reality to the stage. It is a comedy written in poetic dialogue with a romantic flavor. Perhaps its best classification is that of Lorenzo in his prologue to Esteban's play, "a tragedy of laughter and a comedy of tears."

"It is a home-made play such as one can see in any village from Quintana Roo to the Rio Grande. When a Mexican goes to a play he goes, not as a spectator, but with the firm intention of being as much a part of the drama as the actors on the stage. It is the prompter, however, who bears the full burden of the performance, and so, to him, health and wealth.

"All of the characters, with the exception of Mariana, are drawn from life. Esteban, whose real name I have forgotten, I often used to see at dances playing a saxophone which he had bought from a Sears, Roebuck catalogue, because, as he said, it looked so much like a worm. He called it a 'sasafona,' and when he blew into the mouthpiece it rested with God as to what note would come out at the other end.

"Lorenzo, Ester, Don Pepe, Doña Berta, are all people whom I have known and loved since infancy. I can still see in memory the various Esters sitting primly at dances while their fans flashed back and forth in signals at the various Lorenzos grouped about the doors, while the Doña Bertas sat in magnificent grandeur ready to pounce on the first couple which did not behave in a manner befitting young ladies and gentlemen.

"If there is a moral to be found in this play, I think it is this: that we may thank God that there are still grown people who retain the hearts of children."

The Red Velvet Goat was included in The Carolina Playmakers' forty-seventh bill of new plays, "Mexican Night," April 25, 1936.

AZTECA

Azteca endeavours to capture the spirit of the ancient ritual in a pattern of musical sounds.

The scene is the garden of the great temple of the all-powerful deity of the Aztecan pantheon, The Earth Mother. The action takes place one hundred and seven years before the landing of Cortés in Mexico. The author reminds us that men were admitted to the sacred rites of the temple only when they came with a bequest, and that no greater honor could come to a girl than to be chosen as a sacrifice to the Earth Goddess. The play concerns a lovely novice, Xochitl, "a flower with the serene beauty of a white rose. Seeing her, one thinks of a mountain in the far distance—placid and distinct against the sky—yet capable of a dark and terrible aspect with the setting sun."

Azteca was included in the forty-seventh bill of new plays, April 25, 1936, which was given over to Miss Niggli.

SUNDAY COSTS FIVE PESOS

Sunday Costs Five Pesos is a hilarious comedy of small town Mexican folk. The author tells us it is based on an old Mexican law that is still enforced in many of the small villages of the Republic. No one knows the reason for its existence, but its phrasing goes straight to the point: "A woman who starts a fight on Sunday must pay a fine of five pesos." Since Sunday alone is stressed the result is that what fighting is done is generally held over for week days. Five pesos (about one dollar and a half) is a very large sum to pay for the privilege of scratching an enemy's face, especially when you take into consideration that this amount would support a village family for a month.

Sunday Costs Five Pesos was produced originally by The Carolina Playmakers on April 25, 1936 and proved so successful in Chapel Hill that it was included in our repertory and taken on the thirty-fifth tour last fall.

Mexico may well be proud of the achievement of Josephina Niggli in these little plays. They speak for her people with authentic realism and poetic feeling. As Señor Rodolfo Usigli says in his Foreword, "There is a tender touch of smiling maternity in her treatment which gives a peculiar grace to the characters.... Her selection of material is accurate and definitely Mexican."

With a view to establishing a native drama in her own country, Miss Niggli is planning to write, in Spanish, plays for the theatre in Mexico.

It is her hope that these, her first *Mexican Folk Plays* in English, will serve somewhat toward a better understanding of our Mexican neighbors.

F. H. K.

Chapel Hill, North Carolina
March 5, 1938

FOREWORD

As a Mexican author whose lot has been to live in this pioneering period of our native drama I have this regret: that Josephina Niggli has written her plays originally in English. It is not a nationalistic complex which enforces this feeling upon me, but the great desire for new plays that will place our theatre on the same high level as our painting and our lyric poetry.

Mexican folk drama does not really exist. Or rather it does not exist as drama but as a casual cumulation of external, picturesque facts poorly woven into a dramatic plot. In fact drama does not seem to be, up to now, the most adequate literary expression for Mexico.

This might seem a gross misstatement to the American reader who has followed in newspapers, travel books, and innumerable novels written by American authors on fellowship work, the great, colorful and confusing tragedy of the Mexican spirit. The fact remains that throughout four hundred years we are unable to point to more than two or three names of good or tolerable playwrights, whose works, while deserving a place in the Spanish or the universal theatre, have little or no material to offer which might be regarded as essentially Mexican.

What should be considered as essentially Mexican is a maze open for debate. It is possible to account for this four-centuries-old theatrical wasteland by resorting to the bio-olgical phenomena brought forth by the racial mingle-mangle of the colonial period. But, somehow or other, this does not seem satisfactory either. There would be, on one hand, the fatalistic tragedy of the Aztec and other subdued races deprived of their gods and language. On the other hand would be the impulsive, strong, stubborn, steady spirit of Spain. These are good dramatic materials, yet each is apparently neutralized by the other.

I shall not attempt to analyze minutely these origins of our present—a dramatic present without drama, overflowing with an urge for expression.

Unfortunately, the theatre is not profitable for the author in this country. Plays of the commercial theatres are changed weekly, thus depriving the author of all opportunity to be paid for more than a single week's performance, and the actors of all possibility of developing the depth and the reality of their work. Therefore, no ambitious productions are staged. The few exceptions to this tradition are generally alien plays: Spanish, easy to act, operating on the great capacity of our audiences for sentimental stupidity, and furnishing our lazy commercial players with an opportunity to relax in an aimless forgery of dramatic art through the progressive superficiality of slapstick comedy characters.

Having no professional producers, authors can not expect very much from commercial actors, for whom the theatre is daily bread instead of art. This lack of stimulus has proven lethal to our authors. They barge into novel writing, which is easier and more productive. Then there are the authors possessed of a solid literary culture, with a fine language but no knowledge of dramatic technique; as well as authors who have a little shrewdness, who could tell a dramatic effect from a sonnet, but who, somehow or other, do not concern themselves with the essentials of drama and produce eight-day plays, scantily seen and quickly forgotten.

The most successful type of Mexican playwright is the writer of sketches for musical shows called *revistas* which are equally doomed insofar as duration is concerned. But they are infinitely more alive. The *revista* has really been the refuge of popular Mexican themes and types for the past twenty-five years. Yet the appalling bad taste, the cheapness of treatment, the arbitrary vulgarity of language, the monotonous dance of sex and obscenity, have rendered such materials and types utterly inadequate for the legitimate theatre.

We have been wanting for years a playwright who would present folk subjects without overrating the picturesque and the vulgar, and with a sense of what drama technically is. This explains why I do regret that Miss Niggli has written her plays in English. Her name, in this especial province, should be added to such names as those of Celestino Gorostiza and Xavier Villaurrutia, our lyrical dramatists, or Amalia de Castillo Ledón—whose realistic plays on the psychology of Mexican women have outlasted many others on the billboards as representatives of the modern dramatic production of Mexico.

I cannot help thinking, though, that had Miss Niggli written her plays here for our commercial theatres, she would have encountered the obstacles which we are trying at present to overcome, instead of the cordial reception which she found in Chapel Hill. Professor Koch and The Carolina Playmakers have doubtless meant a great deal in Miss Niggli's career as a playwright.

The plays which are to appear in this volume show different angles of Miss Niggli's approach to her subject, and I take it that they constitute her first formal work. One is the humorous angle in which I find her at her best. *Sunday Costs Five Pesos*, *The Red Velvet Goat* and *Tooth or*

Shave correspond structurally to the good old Spanish *saenete* tradition started by don Ramón de la Cruz: brief one-act plays with popular, clean-cut characters, dialogue simple and alive, innocent plot. They are in themselves the casting of a small great world: a domestic world of closed-in horizons, petty superstitions, childish desires; a happy world where simple folk for whom five or ten pesos are a fortune, lead an even life until an incident arises brought forth by love, jealousy, or ambition. Here is the play: a situation in which characters in various circumstances are moved by alternate impulses, so that they are both naïve and shrewd, puerile and worldly.

Miss Niggli's elements are not universally Mexican... she comes from the North of the Republic and uses what is most familiar to her. But her characters contain the essentials of any Mexican small-town folk attitude towards life. And this point being more important than the rest, the topical does not affect the universal psychological movements of the characters in the plays. They would react similarly under different local circumstances.

Miss Niggli does not look upon her people as an eager vivisector, nor with the Shavian mixture of scientific interest and human contempt which is current now in most realistic plays. There is a tender touch of smiling maternity in her treatment which gives a peculiar grace to the characters.

In three plays a certain Northern flavour is evident to me, even though occasionally I can transpose, on reading, some forms of speech which correspond to a language current all over Mexico: images of a universal value in this country.

The Revolution of 1910 has popularized among us the type of the *Soldadera*, the women who followed the armies keeping the canteen, looking after clothing and food and often getting hold of their men's guns when they were shot, to take their places in battle. Songs, popular poetry, *revista* sketches, military anniversaries and women's clubs have seized on every angle of this subject for years. It is, therefore, a difficult one to approach. Miss Niggli's approach is fresh and vitally romantic. She utilizes some of the songs written for the real *Soldaderas* and succeeds in giving this play an interesting atmosphere and a good dramatic tension. Here, again, she uses one of the innumerable themes for Mexican drama which have been neglected or unsuccessfully attacked by some of our contemporary playwrights. Her source is essentially Mexican, but the treatment strikes me in certain ways as a deliberate one, intended for a foreign public. This may be due to the fact that Miss Niggli was writing for an American audience. A point arises here which is worth considering. It is my feeling that, if presented to a Mexican public, the treatment of *Soldadera* would have to be somewhat different to be altogether satisfactory. Yet the handling of the dramatic elements proves Miss Niggli's insight of her craft.

There have been some spasmodic attempts to utilize in romantic operas and plays the material furnished by our archaeological period. The literary production of the Aztecs, as far as it has been possible to compile it, shows a predominance of religious, political, and familiar subjects. The lyric poetry is rare amongst them, with the exception of Netzahualcoyotl's productions. It is easy to feel in the rhythmic lines of *Azteca* that Miss Niggli is familiar with the religious hymns of the Aztecs to the gods and elements. Her play has beauty and sobriety. Once again, her selection of material is accurate and definitely Mexican, and she contrives successfully to include facts springing from history and tradition into a well-built play. It is my impression, though, that the two latter plays mentioned place Miss Niggli in the category of a romantic playwright who is excelled by the freer, more spontaneous and lively author of the comedies. These appeal to me as the children of her most personal vein. She has also written on other historical subjects, such as the outburst of our War of Independence in 1810 and the Second Empire under Maximilian of Hapsburg.

It has been my contention for some time that we will be in no position to promote the advent of a poetic theatre in Mexico so long as we do not have a true realistic drama created by playwrights well possessed of their craft and of the necessities and limitations of the theatre. I will, therefore, take this opportunity to excite Miss Niggli to write something along this line in Spanish to give the contemporary audiences of Mexico an occasion to appreciate her talents and to rejoice at the appearance of a new Mexican playwright.

I must finally say that this pessimistic outline of our past has not cured me of the chronic hope that we will have a great theatre some day in this country. We are trying to create one, and I wish that we had more authors as alert, interesting and eager as Josephina Niggli.

RODOLFO USIGLI
Directing Head of the Theatre of the National University of Mexico

Mexico, D. F.
September 16, 1937

CONTENTS

APPENDICES

LIST OF ILLUSTRATIONS

From photographs of the original productions of the plays, made by Wooten-Moulton, Chapel Hill, North Carolina.

TOOTH OR SHAVE

A MEXICAN FOLK COMEDY

THE CHARACTERS

As originally produced by The Carolina Playmakers at Chapel Hill, North Carolina, on November 13, and played by them on their Northern tour, November 14 to 26, 1935.

ANSELMO, *a barber*	Robert Nachtmann
MARIA, *his wife*	THE AUTHOR
TOMAS, *a carpenter*	Irving Suss
JUANITA, *his wife*	Ellen Deppe

THE SCENE: The street of "Juarez y Maximiliano" in the town of El Carmen, not very far from Monterrey, Mexico.

THE TIME: The Present. An early morning in spring.

THE SCENE

Dawn is spreading its rosy glow across the two houses that make up this end of the street "Juarez y Maximiliano." Those two names are painted in very black letters on the outside of the house of Tomas, *the carpenter. You can tell where his house ends and* Anselmo's *begins, because that of* Tomas, *on the right, is painted bright purple, and that of* Anselmo's *bright pink. Also, on the stoop of* Anselmo's *house are two flower-pots full of flowers, while between the two doors is a bench... not a very grand bench, but still good enough to sit on.*

Tomas *is a carpenter, and therefore over his door is written in large, orange letters the words "THE TRIUMPH OF AMERICA," and under them, in smaller letters, the single word "CARPENTER." Since* Anselmo *is a barber, his sign is red, very red indeed against the pink wall, and his legend reads modestly "THE CONQUEST OF THE WORLD" with the added information that* Anselmo *is a "BARBER AND TOOTH PULLER." Fastened to the wall, just below the name of the street, is a lottery list.*

When we first see the street there is no one in view, but through the door of Anselmo's *house comes* Anselmo *himself with a tin plate filled with beans in his hand. He pauses a moment on the threshold looking up at the sky, yawning and stretching his arms.* Anselmo *was originally intended to be a mountain, but somewhere in the scale of evolution he turned into a man. That is, he can move and talk. His thinking powers have not yet reached the earthquake stage. He is dressed in white shirt and trousers, with a red bandanna handkerchief knotted about his throat. An oblong piece of brilliantly-striped, heavy cloth, with a slit in the center for his head to pass through, hangs from his shoulders to just below his belt 'fore and aft. He wears leather-thonged sandals and no socks. When he speaks he rumbles. So do volcanos.*

With great dignity, for the reason that he is too bulky to move in any other fashion, he comes down the steps and goes around to the gate on the left side that leads into the corral *where he keeps his chickens and his one goat.*

As he does this, his wife MARIA *comes sleepily out, dragging a broom behind her. After a yawn and a glance at the sun, she starts to sweep. She has much patience, by reason of having* ANSELMO *for a husband. Perhaps she is thirty, or perhaps she is forty-five. It doesn't matter. She'll look the same way when she's seventy, her hair screwed up on top of her head and her shoulders swathed in a shawl. What she lacks in elegance of dress she makes up in petticoats, and they flash beneath her pink skirt as she sweeps.*

In a moment the other door opens and JUANITA *comes out with her broom, followed by her husband,* TOMAS. *There is no especial difference between* MARIA *and* JUANITA *in age, but where* MARIA *is stout,* JUANITA *is thin, and where* MARIA *is positive,* JUANITA *is inclined to whine.* JUANITA *can never forget that her brother leads the town orchestra on Sunday.*

TOMAS, *who is busy arranging his carpenter's tools, is small and clever, with the cleverness of all small things that must battle the world with brain instead of brawn. His white trousers and orange shirt are none too clean, and his straw sombrero is often removed so that he can mop his face with a large and brilliantly green handkerchief.*

MARIA (*leaning on her broom handle*). Good morning, Juanita. And to you, Tomás. How goes the world with you today?

JUANITA (*whining*). As usual—not so good as yesterday, and less well than the day before.

MARIA. Precisely. And the cost of corn one cent higher. (*With a disgusted look at* ANSELMO *who is standing just inside the gate, busily eating.*) I tell Anselmo he eats too much anyway.

ANSELMO (*plaintively*). Now, Maria, a man must eat to live.

(TOMAS, *with an amused glance at his friend, wanders over to the lottery list and stands looking at it with great interest.*)

MARIA (*snapping at* ANSELMO). Does he need to eat all day to live?

(ANSELMO *shrugs and disappears into the* corral.)

JUANITA. At what are you staring, Tomás?

TOMAS. At the lottery lists, my turtle. Someone must have tacked them up last night.

JUANITA (*goes and looks at the list, then calls to* MARIA). Have you seen this?

MARIA (*also goes and looks at it*). Ay, it will be a grand lottery.

JUANITA (*reading the announcement with difficulty*). Twelve thousand pesos for the first drawing! That is a great deal of money.

TOMAS (*going back to his tools*). They are selling tickets through all the towns, and even as far as Monterrey.

MARIA (*shakes her head and returns to her sweeping*). But at ten pesos a ticket? Ay, lotteries bring joy to the wealthy.

JUANITA (*with an extra-superior sniffle*). Of course for those who have ten pesos—

MARIA (*her back turned to* JUANITA, *suddenly grins, and her voice is wickedly superior*). But who has in El Carmen? The mayor?

JUANITA (*this is the hour for which she has been waiting all her life*). Perhaps I have.

MARIA (*stares at her in amazement*). You! (*This is too much for her sense of humor, and she laughs helplessly.*) Juanita, where would you find ten pesos?

JUANITA (*with great virtue*). I have saved it. For a whole year I saved it out of the money I gained from the selling of eggs. I would show it to you, all in silver pesos, had I not given it to Tomás to pay for the phonograph.

MARIA. Phonograph? (*She stares at* JUANITA *as though the woman had lost her wits, and sinks down on the stoop of her own house.*) A phonograph.

JUANITA (*enjoying this sensation*). All the way from Monterrey it is coming. This morning it arrives in a little box—*with records.*

TOMAS (*moaning*). This morning.

MARIA (*to herself, because this is a matter to be treated with awe*). A phonograph—that plays.

JUANITA (*goes up to her*). You grind a handle, and stick in a needle, and there is the music. Of course not such grand music as my brother makes with his orchestra on Sundays—but still music.

MARIA (*wistfully*). I've always wanted a phonograph to play in the evenings.

JUANITA. Of course if your Anselmo did not spend so much money in the saloon...

MARIA (*jumping angrily to her feet*). He spends no more than your Tomás! Not as much!

TOMAS. But I have a position to uphold...

JUANITA. After all, he is the brother-in-law...

MARIA AND JUANITA. Of the leader of the Sunday orchestra!

JUANITA (*finishing triumphantly*). Which is more than your Anselmo will ever be!

MARIA (*topping her*). Thank the Blessed Mary and all the saints!

JUANITA (*with a luxurious sigh*). It gives one such a wealthy feeling to spend ten pesos.

MARIA (*who has started sweeping again*). I prefer to save it.

JUANITA. If you have it to save.

MARIA (*whirling on her*). And perhaps I have. But I'll use it to buy me a grand funeral, with a coffin . . . a real coffin . . . painted lavender. Yes, and flowers, a great circle of flowers made of violets with a cross of white gardenias.

JUANITA (*sniffing and a little angry that she had not thought of this herself*). And I suppose you'll have candles at your head and your feet, and wine to serve to the mourners.

MARIA. Yes, and wine! (*She returns to her sweeping.*) I never had any wine to serve them while I was living. I might as well do it after I'm dead.

JUANITA. Well, I have other things to do beside talking to you about your funeral. I have to clear a table . . . for the phonograph.

Josephina Niggli in Festival Dress

(*With this parting fling she goes into her house with an extra flip of her petticoats.* MARIA *angrily runs to the door and snaps her thumb against her teeth. Then she stalks back to her sweeping.*)

TOMAS (*stares at her narrowly for a moment, then asks with hidden interest*). María, do you really have ten pesos?

MARIA. That I have.

TOMAS (*with condemnation of the idea*). And you leave it where Anselmo can find it?

MARIA (*comfortably*). Why not? Anselmo would not dare to take it. He is too much afraid of my anger.

TOMAS (*contemplating the lottery ticket*). Is Anselmo finished with his breakfast?

MARIA (*shrugs*). What is that to you?

TOMAS. I want a shave.

MARIA. A shave costs ten cents.

TOMAS. I will pay you... tomorrow.

MARIA (*holding out her hand*). Today or tomorrow, a shave costs ten cents... today.

TOMAS (*jerking out a coin and slapping it into her hand*). There! Does that satisfy you?

MARIA (*bites the coin to see if it is good, then leans over the gate and calls*). Anselmo! (*She looks at* TOMAS *with disdain.*) You have a customer.

TOMAS. María, have you ever bought a lottery ticket?

MARIA (*starting to enter her house*). With what? The ten cents I gain from fools like you?

ANSELMO (*enters through the gate with a bright, expectant expression on his face*). Tooth or shave? (*Seeing* TOMAS *he adds with disappointment.*) Oh, it is you.

TOMAS (*flatly*). Shave.

ANSELMO (*not giving up hope*). Look, Tomás. For twenty cents I will pull... (*Tries to look in* TOMAS' *mouth, and then taps his own front tooth.*) I will pull that tooth for you.
(MARIA, *interested in this, circles the two men and stands watching them.*)

TOMAS. Of what use would your tooth be to me?

ANSELMO (*startled*). Not mine, yours! Mine is a good tooth.

TOMAS. So is mine. I want a shave.

ANSELMO (*hopefully*). For two pesos I will pull them all out for you.

TOMAS. How could I eat without teeth?

MARIA. I have some false teeth that belonged to my grandmother. They are still good. She only used them ten years.

ANSELMO (*triumphantly*). For two pesos I will pull out all your teeth and give you the false ones for nothing.

MARIA (*angrily*). Give away my grandmother's teeth, and for nothing?

ANSELMO (*pleadingly*). But, my pigeon, is Tomás not our neighbor? Does he not bring me customers?

MARIA. He sends you no more than you send him!
(JUANITA *enters from her house with a tin bucket slung over one arm.*)

JUANITA. I must have the corn ground. Are you going with me, María? It is not everyone who can walk down the street with the owner of a phonograph.

MARIA (*snaps at her*). And it is not everyone who can walk down the street with a woman whose grandmother had false teeth! (*She goes into the house for her own bucket.*)

JUANITA. Poor soul. Do not forget, Tomás, to go after the phonograph.

TOMAS (*mournfully*). I will not forget.
(MARIA *enters with her bucket.*)

ANSELMO. Will you let my María play a record some night?

JUANITA (*with a very superior air*). Perhaps. If I do not like all the records, she can play the one I like the least.

MARIA (*sarcastically*). Thank you, Juanita, for your kindness. (*Sharply to her husband.*) Now get to work, Anselmo. Do not allow Tomás to keep you talking all the morning.

JUANITA. And you also go to work, Tomás. Remember that tomorrow you must take some eggs to my cousin's aunt's brother-in-law.
(*Both women go out, not loving each other.*)

ANSELMO. Do you want a fancy shave, or just a plain every-day one?

TOMAS (*loudly, looking after the women*). A plain one. This isn't Sunday. (*Then softly.*) Besides, I don't want a shave.

ANSELMO (*puzzled*). But you said you did, just now.

TOMAS (*looking after the women*). That shows what a clever man I am. Now María will have no suspicions.

ANSELMO. Suspicions of what?

TOMAS. That I am going to borrow her ten pesos from you.

ANSELMO. But that is impossible.

TOMAS. You know where her money is, don't you?

ANSELMO. It is in her trunk.

TOMAS. And you have the keys to that trunk.

ANSELMO. They are hidden behind our wedding photograph, but...

TOMAS. You can take the money out of the trunk and give it to me. I can pay for the phonograph at the station, and before she would ever miss the money, I will have returned it to you. Then you could put the money back, and who would be the wiser?

ANSELMO (*who is having difficulty with this logic*). But you paid for the phonograph in Monterrey. Why must you pay for it twice?

TOMAS (*patiently*). But I did not pay for it in Monterrey. I told them to send it out here and that I would pay for it at the station.

ANSELMO. Why don't you pay for it? It is your phonograph.

TOMAS. Because I do not have the ten pesos.

ANSELMO. But where is the money Juanita gave you?

TOMAS (*goes over and pats the lottery list with his hand*). You see, Anselmo, I bought a lottery ticket.

ANSELMO (*with experienced foreboding*). Ay, Juanita will not like that.

TOMAS. But I had a dream. I dreamt that St. Gabriel himself told me to buy ticket number 1027 in the lottery.

ANSELMO. I like not these dreams. (*He turns toward the house, then turns back toward* TOMAS.) And even if you won the money, what would you do with it?

TOMAS. I would pay back the ten pesos that I am going to borrow from you.

ANSELMO. But if you do not win the lottery you will not pay it back, eh? And then what kind of a funeral will my María have? And she has always wanted a lavender coffin.

TOMAS (*slyly*). Of course, if you are afraid...

ANSELMO (*trumpeting*). I am afraid of nothing. Am I not the strongest man in the valley?

TOMAS. You are afraid of María.

ANSELMO (*doggedly*). I am not afraid of her. But if she wants a nice funeral, she shall have a nice funeral.

TOMAS (*strolling away from him*). Good morning, Anselmo. I fear that I can hold no conversation with cowards.

ANSELMO (*reaches out and plucks him back*). Who are you to speak of cowards? Have I not killed rattlesnakes with my bare hands? Have I not crushed between my fingers the thousand-legged spider of death? Why, I would not be afraid of Pancho Villa himself!

TOMAS (*grinning*). You were afraid that he was going to hang you during the revolution.

ANSELMO. And perhaps you do not think it is an honor to be hanged by Pancho Villa.

TOMAS (*with a contemptuous shrug*). But hanging is such a poor death. It has no artistry... no drama. It is the death of a clown. Why anyone could be hanged ... even you.

ANSELMO (*puzzling over this*). I don't know...

TOMAS. But to be shot! Ay, that is different. That is the death of a truly great man.

ANSELMO. But when they shoot you they hurt you.

TOMAS. Not if you know how to receive the bullets.

ANSELMO (*doubtfully*). Well... perhaps.

TOMAS. Now if you will just show me the ten pesos, I will instruct you in the proper art of being shot.

ANSELMO (*thinking this over*). But I am not going to be shot.

TOMAS (*pressing his point*). How do you know that? Many men have been shot who never knew that they would enjoy such an honor. And what happened to them?

ANSELMO. What?

TOMAS (*sadly*). They were failures. They could not understand the drama of the occasion. (*Turns away.*) Ay, it is a sad thing not to know how to be shot.

ANSELMO. Do you know this great secret?

TOMAS (*coolly*). Do I not know everything?

ANSELMO (*with awe*). And you would tell it to me?

TOMAS. In return for María's ten pesos.

ANSELMO (*slowly nods his head as he thinks this over, then contemplates a beaming* TOMAS). No! (*Starts to go into his house.*)

TOMAS (*stops him*). Surely, Anselmo, the secrets of a great execution are worth ten pesos.

ANSELMO (*impatiently*). And what if you do not know the secrets, eh? What if I give you the money and you do not know the secrets? Why, all the world would say that this Anselmo was a fool.

TOMAS. But that is not logic, Anselmo. Does not all the world say it anyway?

ANSELMO. It is María's money, and she needs it...

ANSELMO *and* TOMAS. To buy a lavender coffin.

TOMAS. Still, any woman can have a coffin, but not every man knows how to be shot with elegance.

ANSELMO (*with flat certainty*). And neither do you.

TOMAS. Now, Anselmo, how do you like this? I will show you the proper manner of death, and then, when I have proved my knowledge, you can get me the money. Is that not logic? Is that not fair?

Anselmo (*thoughtfully*). It is possible. It is very possible.

Tomas (*full of enthusiasm, begins his little drama*). We will say that this street is the plaza of execution, and that you are to be shot against this wall. (*Points to the right.*)

Anselmo. No! (*Pulls out the bench and sits on it.*) If you want to have an execution, you can be shot yourself.

Tomas (*who had not thought of this angle*). Well... well...very well, I am the victim. (*Goes over to the right and stands facing* Anselmo.) Now I march in between six soldiers.

Anselmo (*with awe*). Six?

Tomas (*grandly*). Usually there are four. With you there would be only four. But me, I am a person of consequence. I would have six soldiers.

Anselmo (*who is a very practical man*). But we have no soldiers.

Tomas (*with disgust at this lack of imagination*). Of course we have soldiers. Did I not make them up out of my brain? They are standing all about me, and (*suddenly pointing to an empty space behind* Anselmo), out there are four more.

Anselmo (*hastily looks behind him, but seeing nothing looks back at* Tomas, *then quickly looks back again to make sure that he really saw nothing. However the greater imagination of* Tomas *has completely overawed him, so he says meekly*). Precisely. Four more.

Tomas (*acting out his words. He is really enjoying himself*). I enter, my hands tied behind my back, my head drooping in sadness.

Anselmo (*interested*). Why?

Tomas. Death is a sad thing, Anselmo. I am sad, but I feel that I must be noble...

Anselmo. Why noble?

Tomas (*beginning to lose his patience*). Because people must always be noble when they are about to be shot.

Anselmo (*who has the research mind*). Why?

Tomas (*screaming with irritation*). The why is of no value! It is enough that they are! (*Clutching at his mood of noble desperation, he walks slowly to the wall and stands facing it, his hands clasped behind his back.*)

Anselmo (*who is much engrossed in this*). Are you still being noble?

Tomas. I am having my hands untied, you fool! (*He suddenly swings about, acting out his words as he speaks.*) I turn around, I throw back my shoulders, I face...

Anselmo (*wanting to help*). Me.

Tomas (*who has decided to ignore all interruptions*). The soldiers who are about to shoot me. Tears come to my eyes. (*His voice trembles.*) I weep because once I led these brave men in battle...

Anselmo (*who knows better*). You were only a foot soldier, not a general.

Tomas (*snapping at him*). I would have been a general if the revolution had lasted long enough.

Anselmo (*pointing out the bitter truth*). It lasted eight years.

Tomas (*taking a deep breath of resignation*). I turn and face these men whom I *might* have led into battle. One of them comes up to me with a handkerchief, but I turn away my head.... I say "No!"

Anselmo (*scandalized*). But that is not polite, Tomás.

Tomas. Does a man who is about to die concern himself with being polite? I nobly refuse the handkerchief, and he bows to my bravery.

Anselmo. Why would he do that?

Tomas (*wildly*). Because only cowards allow their eyes to be blinded from the sight of death.

Anselmo (*meekly*). I am sorry, Tomás. I thought the handkerchief was for you to blow your nose.

TOMAS (*looking at him in disgust*). And to think that you own ten pesos. (*Deciding to make the best of a bad bargain, he continues, and lost in his drama, he builds up to a great climax.*) I stand and face the soldiers... I throw out my chest... the soldiers raise their guns... they point them at me... I put up my hand... I cry "Viva, México!"... again I throw out my chest ... they shoot...

ANSELMO (*helpfully*). Boom!

TOMAS (*collapsing to the ground*). And I fall dead.... (*His legs twitch, his body goes limp.*) Completely dead.

ANSELMO (*after a pause asks in disappointment*). Is that all?

TOMAS (*sits up in surprise and asks with heavy sarcasm*). I suppose that you can die better than I can.

ANSELMO (*standing*). I can die better than you did just then. It is not brave, Tomás, to stand in front of a little gun that goes ping and you fall dead. That is simple. That is easy. But it takes a brave man to die slowly.

TOMAS (*stalks with wounded dignity to his carpentry box and begins gathering up his tools*). I suppose that you would be content with nothing less than cutting... (*He realizes that he has a saw in his hand. For a moment his voice breaks as the great idea dawns. Then a cunning look flames in his eyes.*) Well... than cutting off a man's head.

ANSELMO (*thoughtfully*). Cutting off a man's head?

TOMAS (*goes to him, holding out the saw*). Yes, with a saw ... a saw like this one.

ANSELMO (*cautiously feels the edge of it, then wrinkles up his face in disapproval*). I do not think that would be so grand a death.

TOMAS. How do you know? Have you ever had your head cut off?

ANSELMO (*scratches his head while he tries to remember if he has. Then he says doubtfully*). No.

TOMAS (*triumphantly*). Then how do you know it would not be such a grand death?

ANSELMO. Perhaps you are right. (*With disdain.*) But a saw ... why even being hanged is better than a saw.

TOMAS (*scandalized, his cunning eyes carefully fastened on* ANSELMO'S *blank face*). And what do you know of saws? They have song, they have personality, they have elegance. Anyone can use an axe to cut off a person's head. An axe, pah! What is an axe?

ANSELMO (*willing to contribute something*). An axe is useful in taking the head from a chicken.

TOMAS. Precisely. And what man, if he is a man, would be brother to a chicken?

ANSELMO. That is true.

TOMAS (*sits down on the edge of the bench*). Now you see this very saw? It is the baritone family, the noblest of them all. Why, if this saw were a man, he would be the mayor of El Carmen.

ANSELMO (*who is still to be won over*). I . . . don't . . . know.

TOMAS. If it were a soprano, that would be different. A soprano is too tender, too feminine, too feeble.

ANSELMO (*offering a delightful bit of information*). I sing bass.

TOMAS. But you are not a saw. And even if you were a saw, Anselmo, you would be of no use in the delicate matter of cutting off a man's head. A saw of the bass voice is too stiff . . . too brutal. But a baritone . . . a baritone is the very king of saws. It has tone. It is to the hand as a knife to the butcher. And yet it is as sure, it is as certain, as yesterday. Why, if it were pulled across a man's neck, it would cut the flesh as easily, as smoothly, as the herder cuts the hair from a goat.

ANSELMO. But who would want to have his head cut off?

TOMAS (*with surprise*). You.

ANSELMO (*with even more surprise*). Me?

TOMAS. Certainly. Did you not say yourself that any man could stand up and have a gun go ping at him?

ANSELMO (*who does not like this*). But why should I have my head cut off?

TOMAS (*shrugs*). How should I know that? That is between you... (*with a pious glance at Heaven*) and the blessed saints.

ANSELMO (*who is beginning to get worried*). But, Tomás, you do not understand. I do not want...

TOMAS (*indifferently*). Of course, if you are afraid....

ANSELMO (*with bravado*). I am afraid of nothing. (*Plaintively.*) But María may not like it.

TOMAS. Of course she will like it. She can always find herself another husband.

ANSELMO (*rubbing his throat*). I do not want to speak of this any longer. (*Starts toward his house.*) To me it is not funny.

TOMAS (*catching his arm. In a horrified voice*). Funny? Funny! But this is a serious matter. I never thought, Anselmo, that you would be such a coward.

ANSELMO (*firmly*). I am a man of honor...

TOMAS (*deeply hurt*). Precisely. And yet you are afraid to kneel down and allow me, your old friend, your old neighbor, to saw off your head. I ask you, is that kindness to me?

ANSELMO (*who is now completely out of his depth*). Tomás, one moment. One little moment. Why would your cutting off my head be of service to you?

Tomas. Anselmo, are you a man of brains, or an idiot and a fool? Any carpenter can make doors, any carpenter can saw wood... but it is the test of a great carpenter to saw off a man's head.

Anselmo (*trying to make things clear*). But I can not leave my María.

Tomas. Do you think she would want you after she knew this?

Anselmo (*driven to the end of his endurance*). Knew what?

Tomas (*screaming*). That you were too much of a coward to let me cut off your head.

Anselmo (*knowing he is beaten, yet still trying to fight*). No... no... I am not a coward, Tomás. I am a brave man.

Tomas (*laughs scornfully. He is really enjoying this*). Brave! Brave as the little mouse... brave as the little bird... brave as the little flea! How all the world will laugh at this brave Anselmo!

Anselmo (*blustering*). No man dares to laugh at me...

Tomas. But they will laugh, Anselmo, they will laugh. When you walk down the street, people will laugh. And do you know what they will say?

Anselmo (*in the last torment*). What?

TOMAS (*singing it out*). They will say, "There goes the great barber who was afraid... afraid to have his head cut off!" How will you like that?

ANSELMO (*wailing*). They will laugh at me... at me!

TOMAS (*rubbing his hands together slyly, and bending toward this mountain in distress*). Of course... I need not tell them.

ANSELMO (*staring at him perplexedly*). Eh? What is that? What do you say?

TOMAS (*his voice soft and cunning*). Perhaps I could forget the glory that might have been mine. Perhaps I could forget everything... if you gave me María's ten pesos.

ANSELMO (*looks at him thoughtfully, then, with great effort, shakes his head*). No. No! That money is for my María's funeral... (*He turns and looks down the street toward the mill, then makes the great gesture of his life.*) and I would rather lose my head than face her anger. (*He lumbers over to the bench and kneels down at its end.*) Come, Tomás.

TOMAS (*with horrified amazement, as he realizes that his talent for salesmanship has proved a boomerang*). You mean... you mean that you are going to let me cut it off?

ANSELMO (*with the fatal resignation of an earthquake*). Now.

TOMAS (*making sure*). You mean you want me to cut it off.

ANSELMO. Yes.

TOMAS (*nervously*). But, Anselmo, we do not have to do this today. (*Thankfully thinking of a release.*) Remember, you have a godson in Mina. They are holding the baptism today.

ANSELMO (*with resignation*). I can be there in spirit.

TOMÁS. But a spirit can not make gifts. And of what use is a godfather without gifts?

ANSELMO (*settling back on his heels*). There is logic in that.

TOMAS (*with a relieved grin*). Perhaps we had better not cut off your head today. (*He turns to replace the saw in the box.*)

ANSELMO (*who, having once made up his mind, finds it difficult to change*). No. I have decided. You are going to cut it off today.

TOMAS (*frantically searching for an excuse*). But who would go to the baptism?

ANSELMO. You could go.

TOMAS. Now, Anselmo, that would not be fair to the baby. Already he thinks his name is to be Anselmo. How would he feel if it were changed to Tomás, and without even asking him?

ANSELMO (*measuring a tiny distance between his two great hands*). He is just a little baby. He would not mind.

TOMAS (*growing more and more nervous*). No, no, Anselmo. I do not feel in the mood today. Perhaps it would be better if we left this until tomorrow.

ANSELMO (*who is not to be argued out of it*). Tomorrow you must take eggs to Juanita's cousin's aunt's brother-in-law. I heard her tell you.

TOMAS. Then the next day.

ANSELMO. That will be the drawing of the lottery.

TOMAS. The day after the lottery...

ANSELMO. You will be drunk. You are always drunk after lotteries.

TOMAS. There is still Tuesday...

ANSELMO (*losing his patience*). That is the day of grandfather Devil himself. Do you think that I want to send my soul to hell? (*He stands up and roars.*) Tomás, I have decided. You will cut off my head...now!

TOMAS (*fighting for time*). But first I must examine your neck. Perhaps it is not the kind of a neck for a saw. (*He runs over and jumps upon the bench beside* ANSELMO.) A saw needs a very wonderful neck. (*Sweeping off* ANSELMO'S *hat, he bends the big man's head forward, examines his neck, and then gives a sigh of relief.*) There! I thought so. You have not even a good neck.

ANSELMO (*rubbing it*). What is wrong with it?

TOMAS. It lacks perfection. Is it a good round neck? No! Does it have a little crease in the fold of the flesh at the back? No!

ANSELMO (*trying to digest this*). But for what is the crease?

TOMAS. Where else would the saw rest as gently as a babe in its mother's arms, but in the crease in the back of your neck?

ANSELMO (*flatly*). If you were a good carpenter, a crease would make no difference to you.

TOMAS (*very hurt, steps down from the bench and strolls away from him*). You say that to me . . . to me who am only thinking of you. There are no thanks in you. But how do I know? Perhaps you want the jagged edge of the saw tearing into your flesh.

ANSELMO (*cautiously*). Tearing?

TOMAS. But of a certainty . . . tearing. (*His voice dripping with hidden tortures.*) Pulling your skin to pieces bit by bit.

ANSELMO. But that would hurt.

TOMAS (*forcing his point*). Of course it would hurt! You suffer such agonies . . . aye, Blessed Mary and the Saints! It would be worse than any pain in hell! (*Creeping up on the barber, who retreats, trying to conceal his growing terror.*) Have you ever seen a man who was stung by a tarantula?

ANSELMO (*gulping*). Yes.

TOMAS. It would be a thousand times worse than that. Have you ever seen the victim of a rattlesnake?

ANSELMO (*gulping again*). Yes.

TOMAS. His torment was as nothing to what yours will be. Anselmo, I beg of you, do not make me do this thing to you.

ANSELMO (*whose logic is getting a trifle mixed*). But you said it was for your own glory.

TOMAS. Do not think of me. I will forget my dreams of glory. I... Tomás the carpenter will do that for you, because you are my friend... (*A sob becomes a tremolo in his voice.*) ... my great, good friend.

ANSELMO (*who can no longer understand what anything means. He, also, is almost in tears*). But I can not have all the world laugh at me.

TOMAS (*stops weeping and becomes practical again*). Anselmo, for you I have done so much. And now I will do even more. If you get me María's ten pesos, the world will know nothing...

ANSELMO (*doggedly*). But María's money...

TOMAS (*not giving* ANSELMO *a chance to form the words*). Nothing of the pain that you have escaped. The terrible pain from which I... your friend... have saved you.

ANSELMO. But María's...

TOMAS (*with the last wild inspiration*). Tell me, Anselmo, is María dead?

ANSELMO (*thinking this a very foolish question*). Certainly not. Did she not go down to the mill to have some corn ground for my dinner?

TOMAS. When does she plan to die?

ANSELMO (*with a sigh of resignation*). Not for many years.

TOMAS. Then what need has she now for funeral money? (*He allows this to sink into* ANSELMO's *mind, then adds the final jab.*) Unless she expects to bury you.

ANSELMO (*indignantly*). But I am not dead.

TOMAS. Precisely. And there is that money in the trunk ...ten pesos, ten round silver pesos at which she never looks. Now what harm is there if I borrow it for a few days...just until after the great lottery?

ANSELMO (*scratching his ear, and willing to be reasonable*). That is logic.

TOMAS. And I tell you what I will do. When I win the twelve thousand pesos, I will give you ten for yourself, ten more than I owe you.

ANSELMO (*a grin dawning in his eyes*). With ten pesos I could...

TOMAS (*dangling the bait*). You could buy a goat.

ANSELMO (*seeing the high great dream*). No! Another pair of dentist's pliers.

TOMAS. Now, is that not worth lending me the money?

ANSELMO (*cautiously*). And you promise that you will say nothing to the town about sawing off my head?

TOMAS (*rubbing his palms together in the bargaining spirit*). Well, if I should ever start to forget, you could always buy me a drink at the saloon. A small glass of beer, and my tongue would be silent.

ANSELMO (*making the great decision*). Very well, I will get the money. But you stay out here and watch for María. Oooo, if she should catch us!

TOMAS. I will stand watch, only hurry!

(ANSELMO *lumbers into the house. The moment he is out of the way* TOMAS *blows out his lips with a sigh of relief, gathers together his carpentry tools including his saw and a hammer, replaces the bench against the wall between the two houses, and slides the box beneath it, unwittingly leaving the handle of the hammer sticking out. This done, he takes off his hat, wipes his head with a bright bandanna, and, suddenly realizing that it is time for the women to return from the mill, hurries over and peers down the street.*)

ANSELMO (*calling from inside the house*). I can not find the keys!

TOMAS (*anxiously watching the street*). Of course you can find them. Look for them! Do not stand there bellowing in the middle of the room.

ANSELMO. I found them.

TOMAS (*desperately*). Open the trunk, Anselmo. Open the trunk! I think I see the women coming down the road.

ANSELMO. The key will not turn in the lock.

TOMAS (*jumping up and down*). Try another key! It *is* the women coming! Hurry!

ANSELMO (*projecting his bulk into the street*). I found it.

TOMAS (*snatching the bag of clinking silver pesos from him*). Give me that money. And you come to the station with me. I want you to carry the phonograph. (ANSELMO *obligingly starts down the street toward the left.* TOMAS *clutches the barber by the back of his shirt.*) Why are you going that way? Do you want to meet María face to face? (*Swings the mountain around to face the right.*) We will go this way. (*A thought suddenly strikes him.*) Did you remember to close the trunk?

ANSELMO (*scrooging up his face in an effort to remember*). I don't know. (*Starts toward his house.*) I will see.

TOMAS (*getting in his way*). Not now! It is too late! Run! (*Putting himself behind* ANSELMO, *he places both hands on the barber's back, and pushing as though he were moving a heavy van, finally succeeds in ejecting* ANSELMO *to the right as the women enter from the left.*)

(MARIA, *the bucket of corn balanced on her head, pauses, a suspicious look in her eyes, then she runs to the right with* JUANITA *strolling behind her.*)

MARIA. Was that not Anselmo and Tomás running down the street?

JUANITA (*sniffing*). Do not change the subject, María. You never possessed ten pesos... ten silver pesos all at once in your life.

MARIA (*thoughtfully*). I wonder what they have been doing. Anselmo never runs away from me unless he has been making mischief. (*She turns abruptly and counts her flowers, then shakes her head, puzzled.*) No, my flowers are all here. He has not sold any of them.

JUANITA (*putting her bucket inside the door of her house*). Only rich people can afford to keep ten pesos without spending it.

MARIA (*with growing concern*). Do you think he sold our goat? (*She whirls and runs through the gate into the patio.*) If he has, I will change Anselmo into a goat.

JUANITA (*hangs over the gate*). When poor people like us have such a grand fortune they show it to their neighbors.

MARIA (*enters from the patio*). No, the goat is still there, and all of the chickens, too. What could he have been doing?

JUANITA. Perhaps he borrowed your ten pesos . . . (*flaring out at her*) . . . if you really have it.

MARIA (*conscious of only the last part of* JUANITA'S *sentence, jerks her head triumphantly*). So . . . you think I do not have it.

JUANITA (*with a shrug*). Well, I had heard nothing of this great fortune of yours until this morning. And the possession of ten pesos is not something that one keeps secret.

MARIA (*with decision*). Very well, I will get it and show it to you. (*She starts toward her door, then suddenly pauses and circles back toward* JUANITA. *This is too great a bargaining moment to be lost. With a tantalizing grin, her voice honey-sweet, she says*): Ten, shining, silver pesos.

JUANITA (*surprised at* MARIA'S *sudden change, but suspicious of nothing, merely shrugs*). Me, I have always believed my eyes instead of my ears.

MARIA (*goes to the stoop of her own house and sits down, her skirts spread about her, and queen of the moment*). I do not see why I have to show it to you. What have you ever done for me?

JUANITA. I told you about my phonograph.

MARIA (*taking a cigarette and a match out from behind her ear*). That is a small matter, and of no account. I do not think that I will show it to you after all.

JUANITA (*creeping up on* MARIA, *and offering a tantalizing bait*). I have learned a new stitch in crochet I could teach you . . . one I was not even going to show my sister.

MARIA (*indifferently*). I know more about crocheting than you will ever know. (*She strikes the match on the door jamb, smiling blissfully.*) Ten round, shining, silver pesos, that slip between the fingers, and slide between the fingers . . . like little, happy, silver tears.

JUANITA (*moistening her lips with anticipation*). I will let you hold one of my records in your hands.

MARIA (*almost chanting*). Ten silver pesos with which to buy a coffin . . . a lavender coffin . . . the most elegant coffin in town . . . in the republic . . . in the world! (*She finally applies the burning match to the cigarette.*)

JUANITA (*the bargain forced out of her, almost against her will*). I would even let you put the record on to play, and that is a matter of skill.

MARIA (*dreamily*). Perhaps I shall have a pillow the color of a rose for my head . . .

JUANITA (*adding more to her offer*). Perhaps I would let you grind the handle.

MARIA. And for such a grand funeral even the mayor would come... the mayor of El Carmen himself!

JUANITA (*driven to the last outpost*). You could play a record... any record you liked.

MARIA (*delighted. This was what she was bargaining for*). Aye... that is different! (*Suddenly she realizes her advantage.*) But only one record for the sight of ten silver pesos? No!

JUANITA (*eagerly*). Perhaps even two records.

MARIA (*thinks this over, and then shakes her head*). No. If I can not play all your records... before you do... you see no money.

JUANITA (*flounces away*). Keep your money!

MARIA (*rising and flinging away her cigarette*). Very well. I can look at it. I can look at it all I want to. (*She goes up to* JUANITA *and whispers tantalizingly.*) I can even play with it... build houses out of the pretty, shining pesos. Perhaps I would even let you build houses with them... but, no... (*She turns and strolls back to her house.*) You have to play your phonograph.

JUANITA. I do not think you even have any money, you keep it so well hidden.

MARIA (*gleefully*). And to think that you will never know. Morning after morning you will wake up, and you will never know that right in the next house are ten silver pesos.

JUANITA (*spitefully*). I will know when you are dead and have a great funeral... if you have it.

MARIA (*coolly*). But suppose you die first. Suppose that I wait and let you die first. What then?

JUANITA (*beaten at last*). Very well, you can play the records.

MARIA (*eagerly*). All of them?

JUANITA (*despondently*). Yes.

MARIA. First?

JUANITA (*almost shakes her head, but her curiosity wins the battle*). Yes.

MARIA (*joyfully*). Then prepare yourself... prepare yourself for beauty! (*Catching up her skirts she whirls into the house.* JUANITA *clutches her hands together in anticipation and creeps closer to the door. Suddenly there is a scream from inside, and then* MARIA *runs wildly out to the street.*) It's gone! It's gone! My money! My beautiful money! It's gone!!

JUANITA (*anxiously*). What has happened?

MARIA (*screaming*). My ten pesos... they are gone... they are not here! (*She suddenly realizes the truth, and runs toward the right.*) So that is why Anselmo was running away.

JUANITA (*who can not conceal her joy at* MARIA's *bad luck*). He has probably gone to buy a lottery ticket.

MARIA (*pathetically, realizing that this is exactly the sort of thing* ANSELMO *would do*). And to think that Anselmo took my money, the money for my beautiful, lavender coffin... to buy a lottery ticket. (*With quick anger she whirls on* JUANITA.) He would never have thought of it had it not been for your Tomás.

JUANITA (*injured*). That is right. Blame my Tomás. What more could I expect from the wife of Anselmo, the barber!

MARIA. My Anselmo would never have thought of it alone. Why, he never had a thought in his life. (*She turns and clenches her fist in the direction of the road to the right.*) If I could just reach out and grasp your Tomás right now between my hands.

JUANITA (*catching* MARIA's *shoulder and swinging her about as she screams with anger*). You will grasp no husband of mine!

MARIA (*also screaming angrily*). What care I whose husband he is? (*Jerking free of* JUANITA *she once more looks toward the right, and sees the men coming.*) Ay, there they come now, walking along as innocently as two baby rattlesnakes.

JUANITA (*peering down the street and hiding a grin behind her hand*). Tomás is making your Anselmo carry my phonograph.

MARIA. But which one has my ten pesos? That is the important thing. (*Drawing* JUANITA *with her, she moves toward the left, speaking quickly under her breath.*) Now, Juanita, when they come, you say nothing. I will do the talking.

JUANITA. They have seen us.

MARIA (*disgustedly*). Yes. And see how Anselmo is wiping the sweat from his face, the fat little pig.

JUANITA (*consolingly*). If they have spent your money, María, I will allow you to play my phonograph.

MARIA (*with venom*). Then I will have to play it in the jail. If they have spent it I will surely kill them both. Now, remember, not one word from you.
(*She settles her arms across her chest, and looks a tower of angry silence as the two men enter from the right,* ANSELMO *clutching the portable phonograph up against his chest. Seeing the two women, the men pause abruptly.* ANSELMO, *a little behind* TOMAS, *is like an elephant seeking protection behind a mosquito.*)

TOMAS (*with false brightness*). Here is your phonograph, my pigeon.
(*There is a silence from the women.*)

ANSELMO (*trying to do his bit*). It has records fastened in the top. We looked.
(*Again the awful silence.*)

TOMAS (*nervously*). It is lucky that the station is so short a distance away. The phonograph is heavy. Poor Anselmo could hardly . . . carry . . .

(His voice dwindles into silence as he and ANSELMO, *much to their horror, see* MARIA *start slowly toward them, each slap of her slipper against the hard ground a slap of approaching doom. Reaching* ANSELMO *she comes to a halt and silently extends her hand, palm up.* ANSELMO, *giving a helpless glance from* MARIA *to* TOMAS *and back to* MARIA *again, and not quite knowing what to do with that extended hand, suddenly breaks into a grin. Shifting the phonograph to one arm, he enthusiastically shakes* MARIA'S *hand. With an angry snort she snatches it away from him.)*

MARIA *(starting softly but achieving a crescendo)*. Well, my little red ants...my little, stinging wasps...mud wasps!

ANSELMO *(plaintively)*. But María...

TOMAS *(with practiced innocence)*. Is there something wrong, María? Are not you and Juanita glad to see the phonograph? It has a very elegant case, and...

MARIA *(coldly)*. Where is it?

TOMAS *(delightedly pointing at the phonograph)*. Right here, María.

MARIA *(stretching out her hand to him)*. Give it to me. (TOMAS *takes the phonograph from* ANSELMO *and starts to extend it to* MARIA, *when she speaks again, each word measured doom.)* Not the phonograph. My ten pesos!

ANSELMO (*moaning as he crouches behind* TOMAS). Ahhhhhhh.

TOMAS (*trying to bluff it out*). What ten pesos, María?

MARIA. You know well enough what ten pesos. The ten pesos for my funeral, for my flowers, for my lavender coffin.

ANSELMO. But we do not have your money, my pigeon.

MARIA (*with disgusted resignation*). So, you spent it. Well, give me the lottery ticket.

ANSELMO. I do not have the ticket....

JUANITA. Did I not tell you, María? Anselmo, you should hide your head in shame...to think that you would lie to your good wife.

ANSELMO (*who doesn't want any blame he doesn't deserve*). But I did not buy the ticket. Tomás bought it.

TOMAS (*horrified, and trying to shut* ANSELMO *up*). I bought it! I certainly bought no ticket!

JUANITA (*flaring out at* ANSELMO). So! As usual you try to blame my poor Tomás.

ANSELMO (*who can not understand all this, turns helplessly to* TOMAS). But you told me you had bought a ticket.

MARIA. Tomás, did you buy a lottery ticket with my money this morning?

TOMAS (*virtuously*). I certainly bought no ticket with your money . . . nor this morning.

ANSELMO (*brightly, glad to be able to add his bit to the general knowledge*). Oh, no, María, you do not understand. He bought it in Monterrey last Wednesday with Juanita's money.

TOMAS (*frantically*). Silence, you fool!

JUANITA (*gasping for air*). With my money! Then with what did you pay for the phonograph?

ANSELMO. With María's ten pesos.

JUANITA (*jerking the phonograph away from* TOMAS, *her voice quivering with wrath*). Give me that phonograph and get in the house.

MARIA (*whirling* JUANITA *around and seizing the phonograph herself*). Just a moment! This is my phonograph now!

JUANITA (*dangerously*). Your phonograph!

MARIA (*firmly*). My money paid for it, and I am going to own it.

(TOMAS, *as the women start to argue, realizes this great opportunity for escape, and starts to creep out toward the left, towing* ANSELMO, *who is very much interested in the coming feminine fight, after him.*)

JUANITA (*screeching*). I thought of the phonograph... my Tomás went in to buy it... and it belongs to me!

MARIA (*crushingly*). But now it belongs to me! (*She sees the men edging down the street.*) Where do you two think you are going?

TOMAS (*abruptly stopping*). I was going down to the saloon to tell the village a little tale of Anselmo and his head!

ANSELMO (*wailing*). But you promised me that if I gave you María's money you would not tell them about my head.

JUANITA (*her anger breaking free at last*). You use my money... my money for which I saved a year... twelve long months... to buy a lottery ticket, and then... and then... you think that you will go down to the saloon! Tomás! (*She takes a step toward his cowering figure, and as she does so she catches sight of the hammer that he had so carelessly exposed in the tool box. The next moment her fingers grasp it, and she swings it above her head as she starts toward him.*) You, Tomás!

TOMAS (*his feet coming free from the ground, he knows this is no time for arguments, and he whirls and dashes wildly down the road to the left, shrieking*). St. Mary and the angels!

JUANITA (*plunges after him, shaking the hammer*). You Tomás! (*They can both be heard screeching in the distance.*)

(ANSELMO *has been peering after this exhibition of rage, but now, as* MARIA *slowly starts toward him, he sidles over and begins busily to read the lottery list. Very quietly* MARIA *walks around him and puts the phonograph down to the left of their door, then she straightens and folds her arms.*

MARIA (*calmly*). What is this of your head?

ANSELMO (*turning to her like a child to his mother*). María, I did not want to use your money. He made me give it to him.

MARIA (*firmly*). What is this of your head?

ANSELMO (*taking off his hat and pulling it between his fingers*). He said I was afraid of you, and I said I was not afraid of anything... of not even having my head cut off... and then he wanted to cut it off, and when I said no, he said he would tell the village and then all the world would laugh at me. So he said if I gave him the money he would not tell the village, and so, you see, I had to give it to him. It would be a terrible thing, María, to have all the world laughing at me for being a coward.

MARIA (*advancing on him as he retreats*). You fool, you idiot, you seven-headed fishing worm!

ANSELMO (*pleadingly*). Now, María, do not be angry with me. Or would you rather that I did have my head cut off?

MARIA. He was not going to cut off your head! Do you think he wanted to be hanged...for murder?

ANSELMO (*blankly*). Hanged?

MARIA. Do you not see that if he had cut you in two you would have been dead? Completely dead?

ANSELMO (*light breaks across the mountain range*). Then it was only a trick...to get your money.

MARIA (*whirls away from him, exasperated beyond her long years of patience*). Anselmo, at times I am glad you have no brains, and at others I could cut off your head myself!

ANSELMO (*slowly, beginning to comprehend*). And all the world would not laugh at me?

MARIA. They might laugh at you for being a fool, Anselmo, but not at your being a coward.

ANSELMO (*his jaw tenses, his great body begins to shake, and hidden anger starts to bubble out of him*). Ahhhhh....

(TOMAS *chooses this unfortunate moment to dash in from the right, having run completely around the block. He is exhausted, between the exercise and his fear of* JUANITA.)

TOMAS (*panting*). María, hold Juanita. I can not run much farther.

(*He tries to run past them, but* ANSELMO *simply*

reaches out his arm and stops him. TOMAS *pulls and tugs, but mountains have a stationary air about them.*)

TOMAS (*fear in his voice*). Let go of me, Anselmo. Juanita is coming.

ANSELMO (*shaking him as an elephant shakes a mouse*). So you would play tricks with this Anselmo, eh?

TOMAS (*trying to jerk free*). Let me go!

ANSELMO (*trumpeting his wrath*). So all the world would laugh at me because I am a coward.

TOMAS (*almost on his knees*). The world will know nothing if you will only let me go. (*Slumps down in terror.*) Here she is!
(JUANITA *runs in, shaking the hammer.*)

JUANITA. There you are! Thank you, Anselmo. Stand out of the way, so that I can make a surer blow.

ANSELMO (*flinging her back with his free arm*). Woman, stand back. This is a man's business.

MARIA (*frightened*). Anselmo, remember, you are very strong.

ANSELMO. So all the world would laugh at me, eh? (*Shakes* TOMAS.) All the world is going to laugh at you, my friend, when they see you without any teeth.

TOMAS (*screams*). Ahhh....

JUANITA (*tugging at* ANSELMO *and screaming in fear*). You stay away from him! He is smaller than you!

ANSELMO (*sweeping her out of the way*). Out of my way, woman!

MARIA. Take care, Anselmo. (*Excitedly to* JUANITA.) I've never seen him this angry but once before in my life, and that was when he threw my father out of the window.

TOMAS (*wildly*). For the love of the saints, Anselmo.

ANSELMO. For the love of my honor. (*With harsh dignity.*) María, bring me the pliers.

TOMAS (*wailing*). No! Juanita, do something!

JUANITA. Anselmo, you leave my Tomás alone. (*Pleading.*) I will let you play the phonograph.

ANSELMO (*grimly*). María will let me play her phonograph.

MARIA (*offering a substitute*). Perhaps you had better wait to pull his teeth when you are a little calmer, Anselmo.

ANSELMO (*roaring*). Bring me the pliers!

MARIA (*looks at them all hesitantly*). Yes, Anselmo. (*She moves slowly toward the house.*)

ANSELMO (*with a louder roar*). María!

(MARIA *jumps as though she had been shot and scuttles into the house.*)

JUANITA. Anselmo, Tomás would look such a fool without his teeth. All the world would laugh at me for having such a husband.

ANSELMO. He would not look so foolish as I without a head.

TOMAS (*whimpering*). But it was only a little joke. All the world will laugh at you for not being able to understand a little joke.

ANSELMO (*tossing* TOMAS *down on the bench*). They will forget about me when they see you. (*He lets out a sudden yell.*) María!

MARIA (*appears in the doorway, her hands behind her back. She gulps*). Anselmo, I could not find the pliers.

ANSELMO. You will find me the pliers, or I... (*He sees the hammer in* JUANITA's *nerveless hand and snatches it away from her.*) ... or I will knock his teeth out with this!

(*He swings it up into position,* TOMAS *shrieks and covers his mouth with both hands,* JUANITA *wails and shrinks back, and* MARIA, *with a scream, jumps down from the steps, covers her face with one arm, and extends the pliers with the other.*)

MARIA. Here they are, Anselmo.

ANSELMO (*snorts, tosses the hammer aside, takes the pliers, and gets down to business*). Open your mouth.

TOMAS (*moaning*). Anselmo, use reason.

ANSELMO. How can I pull your teeth with your mouth shut? Open your mouth!
(TOMAS *shuts his mouth as tightly as he possibly can.* ANSELMO *tickles him,* TOMAS *gives a startled shriek, and* ANSELMO *grips a front tooth with the pliers.* ANSELMO *puts one foot on the bench, his hand presses down the shoulder of* TOMAS, *and just as he starts to give a mighty heave, the church bell slowly begins to toll in the far distance.*)

JUANITA (*with a relieved wail*). The bell for mass! Anselmo, the bell for mass!

ANSELMO (*straightens*). Mass. Mass?

MARIA (*forcing a grin*). Yes, Anselmo, it is time to go to mass. You can not pull teeth, Anselmo, when it is time to go to mass.

TOMAS (*who has taken advantage of this opportunity to get the pliers out of his mouth, adds his argument*). This is time for prayer, not business.

MARIA (*picking up the phonograph and holding it out where* ANSELMO *can see it*). We will take the phonograph and have it blessed. *Our* phonograph, Anselmo.

TOMAS. Yes, *your* phonograph.

JUANITA (*angrily*). His, indeed! It is mine!

TOMAS (*with a warning gesture to his wife*). Silence, you fool. (*To* ANSELMO.) Juanita and I will give you the phonograph in exchange for my teeth.

MARIA. Surely that is fair, Anselmo. We can play it in the evenings when your day's work is done. Is that not better than pulling teeth, Anselmo?

TOMAS. You will be the only man in the village to own a phonograph. Why, not even the mayor has one.

ANSELMO (*begins to beam. Coming to* MARIA *he takes the phonograph from her, as though it were a favorite child*). Yes... *our* phonograph.... (*He looks up and sees the three faces intently watching him.*) Why are you women standing there? Get your veils. We must not be late, or the priest will not have time to bless our phonograph.

MARIA (*with a triumphant grin at* JUANITA *as she sweeps into her house*). Yes, Anselmo.

JUANITA (*sulkily, with a glare for* TOMAS). Yes, Anselmo. (*She, too, goes into her house.*)

TOMAS (*now that the danger is past, his spirits have rebounded to normal. He goes over to* ANSELMO). Perhaps, after the mass, when the women have come home, you and I could stop in the saloon and celebrate the coming of a phonograph to El Carmen. Perhaps you can even buy us a large glass of beer in celebration... ten cent glasses.

Scene from Tooth or Shave

ANSELMO: Open your mouth. How can I pull your teeth with your mouth shut?

ANSELMO (*to whom it does not occur that he is to pay for the celebration*). Yes. Large ones. With foam.
(*The women now appear in their respective doorways, draping their black lace shawls over their hair.*)

MARIA (*with a grin at* JUANITA). Carry the phonograph, Anselmo.

ANSELMO. Yes, my pigeon.
(*He and* TOMAS *start out to the left,* TOMAS *with an anxious glance over his shoulder for* JUANITA *who glares at him. As* JUANITA *reaches* MARIA'S *door,* MARIA *steps down in front of her.*)

MARIA (*with deadly sweetness*). Juanita, in case there is a record I do not like, perhaps I will allow you to play it.
JUANITA *tosses her head and strides past her, with* MARIA *strolling along, a satisfied smile on her face as*

THE CURTAINS CLOSE

SOLDADERA
(SOLDIER-WOMAN)

A PLAY OF THE MEXICAN REVOLUTION

THE CHARACTERS

As originally produced by The Carolina Playmakers at Chapel Hill, North Carolina, on February 27, 28 and 29, 1936.

THE RICH ONE, *a prisoner*	Robert du Four
MARIA, *the sentinel*	THE AUTHOR
THE BLOND ONE, *the ammunition guard* . . .	Christine Maynard
CRICKET, TOMASA } *soldaderas*	{ Phoebe Barr, Jessie Langdale
ADELITA, *a young girl*	Barbara Hilton
THE OLD ONE	Mary Lou Taylor
CONCHA, *their leader*	Gerd Bernhart

THE SCENE: A pass in the Sierra Madre Mountains, near the capital city of Saltillo in the northern state of Coahuila, Mexico.

THE TIME: Early morning in the spring of the year 1914.

THE SCENE

A soldier's camp in the year 1914 in the Sierra Madre Mountains near the capital city of Saltillo in the northern state of Coahuila, Mexico. It is really a mountain pass, and there is a path that begins at the rear right and leads up and out left.

The rocks are rugged spikes of stone against the dark blue sky. Here is no flowery green softness, no delicacy of outline, but a grim fortress built by nature against the valley below. What vegetation exists is sparse and scattered. Perhaps a yucca palm stands aloof from the organ cactus that rears its head above its two vertical bent arms. A maguey *thrusts up its pointed leaves here and there, while small round cacti, studded with thorns, wear scarlet flowers for crowns.*

In daylight the rocks are gray, but the early morning mist turns them to sapphire, brushing the tips with bronze and gold.

It is that hour just before dawn, that hour when even nature itself seems to be asleep, and the only moving thing in all that silence is the figure of a woman standing on the high rock that shields a part of the path from view. Her name is MARIA, *and she is a sentry. In her hand, the butt resting on the ground, is her gun. Her clothes are dirty and ragged, and as a protection against the cold moun-*

tain air she has drawn over her head and shoulders a fringed shawl. As a further protection she wears a man's sombrero.

The stillness of the hour seems to have placed her, too, under a spell, and she stands there like a bronze image, gazing off into the distance at the left.

Below her in the pass are the sleeping figures of other women, the tousle-headed BLOND *stretched out in front of the cave's opening on the left, and the woman known as* CRICKET *bundled up in what was once a blanket, in front of the built-up fire. The middle-aged woman named* TOMASA *is sitting there with her back against the sentry rock at the back. Sleep has toppled her body sideways, but her arm is curved in her lap as though to protect the head that rests there, the head of the youngest of them all,* ADELITA. *She is the poetry of the Revolution, and the beauty, and she who has seen almost nothing of death finds life very gay.*

After a moment, MARIA *looks down at the women she is guarding, and then after a glance up at the sky to see the first pink wisps of dawn draped across the mountains, she allows herself a little moment of rest. Slowly lowering herself to her haunches, she rests her gun across her lap and dares to snatch at forbidden sleep.*

Again there is silence, as though MARIA'S *movements had desecrated a holy service, and then, out of the shadows to the right, steals a figure of a young man . . . a man whose shirt, once white, is now dirty and torn, whose trousers look as though they had been slept in for days.*

He moves slowly, cautiously, seemingly fearful of disturbing the women. As he approaches the path the reason for his caution is revealed. His hands are tied behind his back. Every step he takes forward is a new adventure.

Now and then he pauses to look over his shoulder toward the right, about him at the women, above him at the motionless MARIA. *Very quietly he moves up the path, holding his breath as he creeps past her, and with his head turned toward her he works his way up, and so out of view.*

He is hardly gone from sight before MARIA *begins to raise her head, a grim smile on her face. In a single movement she rises to her feet, and her gun swings up to her shoulder. Carefully sighting down the barrel, she calls out suddenly, raucously.*

MARIA. Look behind you, tenderfoot! (*The echo of her words and the shot come at the same time. She turns her head and spits.*) I can't even shoot a Rich One in the back!

(*Instantly there is confusion in the path. The women, startled into consciousness, are swaying back and forth, almost as though they were drugged. Their voices come in confused shouts.*)

THE BLOND ONE. A shot. I heard a shot! Get up you... Cricket!

CRICKET (*still dreaming. She is the only one who has not moved*). Kiss me again, you brown-eyed devil, or I'll break my knife off in your stomach.

TOMASA (*excitedly to the sentry*). Is it Concha coming home at last, María?

MARIA. No. I just shot our little wealthy pig. You, Cricket and Adelita, go down and get him. He's all crumpled up on the path.

ADELITA (*crying anxiously as she runs up to* MARIA). You didn't kill him!

MARIA (*patting her on the shoulder*). No. I only shot him in the shoulder. Didn't I promise Concha not to kill him until she came back from taking the ammunition to Hilario? You run down and help bring him in.

ADELITA. Oh, the poor man. (*She runs off up the path.*)

MARIA (*shrugging her shoulders*). Our Adelita has the heart of a young hen. Blondie, wake up the Cricket.

THE BLOND ONE (*goes over and looks down at* CRICKET, *then kicks her*). Wake up. Dream about your lovers some other time. (*Kicks her again.*) Wake up I tell you.

CRICKET (*starting up*). What in the name of... He was just buying me a bottle of *mescal*.* A whole bottle.

THE BLOND ONE. María's just shot the Rich One. She wants you to help Adelita bring him in.

CRICKET (*shaking herself awake*). Why does she have to shoot him when I'm having a pleasant dream? (*She goes muttering up the path and disappears at the left.*)

TOMASA (*coming down to the fire*). If we'd killed him when Concha first brought him in we could have slept for another hour this morning.

* *Mescal* is a colorless liquor made from the sap of the *Maguey* cactus.

Maria. Tomasa, you go find out if he slit The Old One's throat for her.

Tomasa. Why don't you send Blondie? I'm an old woman, I am.

The Blond One (*who has gone back to the mouth of the cave*). That's a fine way to talk. Didn't Concha tell me to guard this ammunition? What if one of the bombs should fall out of the box? Do you want to be blown to hell before we shoot all the Federals? (*She spits.*) The mangy blood-drinking dogs.

Tomasa (*whining*). I'm an old woman, I tell you. (*Nevertheless she goes off into the shadows at the right.*)

The Blond One (*digging down into her loose dirty blouse and pulling out a package of cigarettes. As she takes one out she shows the pack to* Maria). Look what he gave me yesterday. He wanted me to help him get away. I told him all right, and then I tied him up tighter to his tree. (*Both the women laugh.*)

The Blond One (*as she lights the cigarette, she asks curiously but without much concern*). I wonder if he did kill The Old One?

Maria (*shrugs*). What is the difference? All she did was grumble anyway. If Hilario didn't have such a kind heart he'd have gotten rid of her long ago. (Cricket *and* Adelita *now come into view. They are supporting* The Rich One *between them. Although he possesses a name, he is called* The Rich One *by the women, since he represents the hated upper-class which has held them in subjection for so long.*)

Adelita. You almost killed him, María.

Maria. Rich Ones have as many lives as a monkey. Why don't you roll him down the hill? It would be easier. (*She steps in front of them.*) The next time, Rich One, I'll put a bullet through that piece of black liver you call a heart.

Cricket. He's heavier than the hand of God.

Adelita (*gently, to* The Rich One). Put more weight on me.

(Tomasa *has entered, and she is watching the procession from beside the glowing fire.*)

Tomasa. He'll be all right, Adelita, if you let him look at his pretty face in the mirror Cricket got for him. (*All the women think this is a great joke . . . all but* Adelita.)

Cricket. Adelita will wash your shoulder for you, Rich One. You won't feel the pain then.

(*She reaches out and slaps him across his wounded shoulder.* The Rich One *gives a sharp moan of pain and flinches back.* Adelita *swings around in front of* Cricket.)

Adelita (*angrily*). What are you doing! You let go of him; I'll take him.

(*She pushes* CRICKET *out of the way, and, putting* THE RICH ONE'S *unwounded arm over her shoulders, she supports him off into the shadows at right.*)

CRICKET (*after a pause*). Our little Adelita is angry with us, my pigeons.

THE BLOND ONE. Perhaps she thinks we ought to give our prisoners a bed made of feathers, and a gay, striped blanket from the factory down in Saltillo.
(CRICKET, *her hands on her hips, strolls to the right and stares after* ADELITA *and* THE RICH ONE.)

MARIA. Well, Tomasa, is The Old One dead?

TOMASA (*putting an iron kettle on the fire*). Not unless the dead can snore. I tried to wake her up, but she had too much *mescal* last night.

THE BLOND ONE (*indifferently*). Oh, well, it keeps her from thinking about her son.

TOMASA. I had a son, too, but I don't want to forget him.

MARIA. You don't let us forget him either.

CRICKET. What do we care about your son?

THE BLOND ONE. Why don't you let our memories alone? We don't want to think of them.

TOMASA (*clutching* THE BLOND ONE'S *arm*). I want to think of him all the time, and every moment I think of him, I want to have a Rich One between my hands.

MARIA (*sharply*). You keep away from this Rich One until Concha comes back. You know what a temper she's got if she finds we haven't done what she told us to do. Why, she'll beat up the lot of us.

TOMASA (*sullenly*). I haven't touched him, have I?

THE BLOND ONE. Anyway she told us we could have this Rich One, and Hilario would never do that when he was here.

(THE OLD ONE *shambles in from the right. She is a very old woman who has seen too much of death, but still she clings to life with the hope burning in her... the same hope that burns in all these women... that this time the Revolution must succeed.*)

THE BLOND ONE. Who woke you up, Old One?

THE OLD ONE (*wiping her face with the back of her hand*). Adelita threw water in my face. These young girls don't know how to respect age any more. (*Looks up at* MARIA.) Well, do you see anything? María! You, Sentinel! Do you see anything!

MARIA (*behind whom the sun is spreading a warm red light*). Nothing. Nothing but cactus and yucca trees ...and the mountains across the valley.

THE BLOND ONE (*to* THE OLD ONE). When do you think Hilario will come back?

THE OLD ONE. When he wins a battle.

CRICKET (*wanders down to the fire*). When he wants to see Concha . . . the hell-cat.
(*All the women laugh.*)

THE BLOND ONE. Cricket is jealous. She would rather have Hilario than the common soldier she's got.

CRICKET (*disdainfully*). And perhaps you think I could not have Hilario if I wanted him.

MARIA (*laughs*). Roll the eye at him and Concha would tear out every hair in your head.

THE OLD ONE (*holding up her thumb*). Not our Concha. She has no need to fight for her men. One shrug of her shoulders, one swirl of her skirt as she dances, and even Cricket's common soldier would slit his own gullet for her.

CRICKET. I can dance too.

THE BLOND ONE (*sneers*). Perhaps you can dance better than Concha.

CRICKET. The men would be slitting each other's gullets for me.

MARIA. You never could dance.

CRICKET. I'll show you.
(*Her foot slaps the ground, her fingers grasp the folds of her skirt, and as she begins to dance* MARIA *mockingly sings LA CUCARACHA.*)

Maria.

> One thing always gives me laughter,
> Pancho Villa * the morning after.
> Ay, there go the Carranzistas...
> Who comes here?

The Other Women (*joining in the chorus*).

> Why the Villistas.
> Ay, Pancho Villa, ay Pancho Villa,
> Ay, he can no longer walk.
> Because he lacks now, because he has not
> Any drug to help him talk! Ay-yay!

(Cricket *finishes triumphantly in front of* The Old One.)

---

* Pancho Villa was the leader in the north of the Agrarian Revolution of 1910. His followers were called Villistas. He was opposed to the government of Venustiano Carranza whose followers were known as Carranzistas.

THE OLD ONE (*grinning with tightly closed mouth and nodding her head*). When Concha returns, perhaps she will teach you how to really dance.

(CRICKET *spits at her, goes back to the fire, and flops down on the ground.*)

TOMASA (*pointing toward the cave left*). What does Hilario care about women? He'll come back when he needs bullets.

THE OLD ONE. Ay, there's the answer. He won't let us fight any more, but we're good enough to mold his bullets for him.

MARIA. And guard his ammunition for him.

CRICKET. And keep a prisoner for him.

THE BLOND ONE (*meaningly*). Leave that to Adelita.

THE OLD ONE (*startled at* THE BLOND ONE'S *tone*). What's that? What did you say about Adelita?

MARIA. Nothing, nothing at all. They were just talking. Words as large as a barn door and full of holes as a cheese.

THE OLD ONE. Has she been talking to that wealthy pig? (*Spits and wipes her mouth with the back of her hand.*)

MARIA. The joke of it is that he doesn't like being called a wealthy pig.

TOMASA. He wears silk next to his skin, doesn't he?

The Blond One (*holding up a package of cigarettes*). And smokes paper cigarettes.

Cricket (*teasing* The Old One). And kisses a lady's hand. You ought to see him kiss Adelita's.

The Old One (*shuffles up to* Cricket). What did you say?

Maria (*raises her gun*). You, Cricket, down there. Keep your mouth shut, or I'll shut it for you.

Cricket (*whiningly*). I'll talk if I want to... about any rich corn-rustler.

The Old One (*goes to* The Blond One). What about Adelita and this man?

The Blond One. Well, what can you expect in five days? Is she not the youngest in the camp? Yes, and the prettiest, too? And he's a very handsome young man. For them to stay apart would be against nature.

Tomasa. He reads to her, too. And he's teaching her her letters. Oh, our Adelita will soon be a fine lady in silks and in laces....

Cricket. And will turn up her nose at the camp.

Tomasa. Imagine. He told Blondie over there she ought to teach the rest of us to talk like ladies.

The Blond One (*slaps her knee*). He thought his sweet words would buy his freedom from me.

Maria. Perhaps he feels it is not manly to be captured by a woman.

Cricket. But it took courage, you must admit that. I feel proud of myself.

Maria (*laughs*). You. You! When all the world knows that Concha brought him in.

Tomasa. With the point of her knife in his back.

The Old One (*disregarding the others and looking to the right where* Adelita *and* The Rich One *are. Swaying back and forth, she is moaning to herself*). Adelita... with a Rich One... a Rich One.

Cricket (*to the others. No one is paying any attention to* The Old One). You needn't worry. This louse won't live long after Concha gets back. (*She sighs.*) It is a sad thing, too. He has a lively eye in his head.

Maria (*slowly*). *If* Concha gets back. She's been gone five days. Hilario wouldn't keep her this long.

Tomasa. Perhaps he's showing her the new way of hanging.

The Blond One. I'd like to see one of those hangings. I've only heard about them.

Tomasa. They tie their ankles together with the same rope that makes a noose around their necks, and then dangle them from a tree limb. As long as they keep their feet pulled up, they live... but once they straighten out... (*Draws her finger across her throat, then points to heaven and laughs.*)

CRICKET. I heard one of them stayed alive three days.

MARIA. It's still too easy a death for them.

THE OLD ONE (*shuffling back to the fire, her shawl wrapped around her. Her voice is dead*). A thousand years in hell would be too easy for them.

CRICKET (*slaps* THE OLD ONE *on the back*). Listen to The Old One. Hilario should have you on his staff to tell him how to get rid of these Rich bastards.

THE OLD ONE (*jerking away from her*). Who has a better right than I? Who has suffered more than I have?

THE BLOND ONE. Now, Old One, we all know the story.

THE OLD ONE (*her voice rising to a crescendo. The mere thought of* ADELITA *being attracted to a Rich One is too much for her*). Sometimes in the night I wake up and hear him crying for me... small mother, small mother! ... until I have to cover my ears and scream to God. (*Rocks back and forth.*) When those Federals took him away I ran after them until I fell to the ground, and then I crawled on my knees for miles and miles until the dear Virgin sent sleep to cover me. Oh, Holy Angels... Oh, Blessed Child of God!

TOMASA. They took my son, too.

THE OLD ONE (*as if she were seeing enacted in front of her this story out of the past. The spell of common suffering has bound the women's attention to her*).

When I had reached the place, they had crucified him... put nails through his hands and fastened him against a door. He was looking up at heaven... I closed his eyes, and then his head drooped down as though he were hunting for my breast. Like a little baby he was...

TOMASA (*laughs grimly*). They were good to my son. They gave him ten paces ahead of a starved pack of dogs. When I found him there was nothing left but the bones. The little Rich squirts told me to make soup out of them.

CRICKET, THE BLOND ONE, AND THE OLD ONE. Oh, Holy Virgin...

MARIA AND TOMASA. Oh, Mother of God.

ALL. Have pity on us.

THE OLD ONE (*shaking her clenched fist above her head*). If Adelita wants a Rich One...
(ADELITA *comes in from the right. As she walks, her skirt swings from side to side and she is lightly humming the ADELITA.*)

THE OLD ONE. Ay, so here you are, my pretty. Was it hard to tear yourself away from his arms?

ADELITA (*startled*). What are you talking about? Why are you all staring at me?

CRICKET. It is not every woman who can boast of a wealthy lover.

ADELITA. He's not my lover!

(*They glare at each other.* MARIA *suddenly jerks her head and yells at* ADELITA.)

MARIA. Where is the Rich One?

ADELITA. He's asleep.

MARIA. And you left him unguarded?

ADELITA (*flinging out her hands*). He is wounded. He cannot escape. And, besides, the cliffs are too high around him. There's no way for him to escape except through here.

MARIA (*relaxing*). I don't trust these Rich Ones, even when I'm looking at them. Old One, you go and watch him.

THE OLD ONE. Why does it always have to be me?

MARIA (*raises her gun*). You heard me.

THE OLD ONE. I'm going. I'm going. (*She disappears right.*)

ADELITA. Can't you give the man a moment's peace? After all, he's human.

THE BLOND ONE. No Rich One is human. They are beasts, all of them.

ADELITA. This man is different. He believes in the Revolution. Why, he even knows the words of the *ADELITA....*

TOMASA (*sneers*). What does he know about the great song of the Revolution?

ADELITA. He's crazy about the Revolution and he wants to know all about us, what we think about, how we live, everything.

MARIA. And I suppose you tell him everything, eh? Not that the news will do him any good, when he's dead.

ADELITA. He says that if he hadn't sworn an oath to the Federals, he'd like to join Hilario.

THE BLOND ONE. So he tells you that, eh? That eater of cow's meat.

MARIA (*jibingly*). And she believes him.

ADELITA. Why shouldn't I believe him? What do you know about him? Any of you? You've never spoken to him . . . not seriously you haven't.

CRICKET. Didn't I capture him?

ADELITA. You? It was Concha.

THE BLOND ONE. Even the infant knows the truth of that story, my Cricket.

CRICKET (*defending herself*). Well, I found him . . .

MARIA. So you say . . .

CRICKET. He was standing by a tree in our territory.

TOMASA. And you went up to him, I suppose, and said, "Rich One, you are my prisoner."

CRICKET. I shot his hat off his head.

TOMASA (*laughs*). I wish I could have heard our Cricket squeak for help when he turned to face her.

CRICKET (*springs at her*). I'll teach you to watch your tongue.
(*They begin to fight.*)

THE BLOND ONE (*seizing hold of* CRICKET *and pulling her back*). You can't fight on an empty stomach.

ADELITA (*trying to hold* TOMASA). Now, Tomasa, remember, you are an old woman.

CRICKET (*spitting at* TOMASA). You cross-eyed shrew!

TOMASA. You monkey's wench!

CRICKET. I'll scratch out both your eyes!
(*Her surging movement forward is arrested by the sound of a woman's voice in the far distance to the left, singing. It is* CONCHA *returning.*)

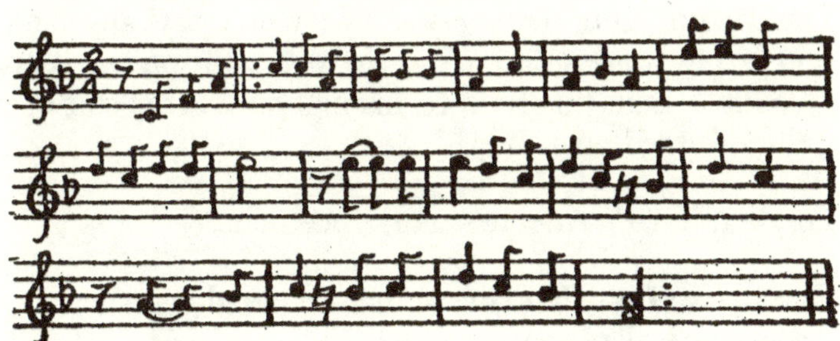

CONCHA (*off left*).

If Adelita should go with another,
If Adelita should leave me all alone,
I would follow in a boat made of thunder,
I would follow in a train made of bone.*

MARIA (*raising her gun*). Concha comes! Back to your post, Blondie! If Concha finds out you left those bombs unguarded, she'll tear out your heart to see it wiggle. (*Turns to the left and waves her arm above her head.*) Concha! Concha!

CONCHA (*still off left, but coming nearer, she calls*). O-la! O-la!

ADELITA (*calls joyfully as she runs up the path*). Concha! (*She runs off to meet her.*)

MARIA (*looking down at the women*). The first one that opens her mouth to Concha about Adelita and that Rich One will get a bullet through her head... from this gun.

* The *ADELITA* was one of the great songs of the Revolution and has over 100 known verses. It holds the same place that *Annie Laurie* did to English soldiers during the World War.

The Blond One (*sullenly*). We won't say anything. (*Putting some beans from the pot on a plate.*) You, Tomasa, take this food to his highness... the son of a three-legged goat.

Tomasa. That's Adelita's work, not mine.

The Blond One. You heard me! Or would you rather I threw the plate in your face?

Tomasa. All right. (*She takes the plate with poor grace and goes out right.*)

(*There is a moment's silence, during which* The Blond One *goes over and squats in front of the cave, then* Adelita *and* Concha *enter down the mountain path at the left.* Maria *has stepped back to make way for this woman-leader. As dirty as the rest of them, there is strength that flowers in her body and sets her above and beyond them. Born of the earth, it is the earth's pulse that she has for her heart. She is the one who keeps these fighting, snarling women together... who can punish with a sure, cold hand, but at the same time can heal their wounds. As merciless as the wind and rain, she is as warm and healing as the sun.*)

Maria. Thanks to our Lady of the Mountains for your return, Concha.

The Blond One and Cricket. May the Saints pour blessings on your head, Concha.

Concha (*her arm around* Adelita's *waist, smiles at the women as a mother smiles at her children*). Hilario sends you many greetings and the news that he has killed a hundred Rich bastards.

ADELITA. Now the Revolution will soon be over.

CONCHA (*as she comes down the path*). Perhaps today, perhaps tomorrow...perhaps a hundred years from now. Ay, the Revolution is a glorious thing. But these bones of mine are weary. (*Looks about her.*) Where is The Old One? Has she no food for me?

THE OLD ONE (*coming out of the shadows at right*). Beans and rabbit stew. Cricket has had good hunting since she found The Rich One. He has put courage in her. (*She starts to fill a plate for* CONCHA.)

MARIA. I killed that rabbit.

CRICKET (*wrathfully*). Is all the world going to take credit from me? Can't I even kill a rabbit?

CONCHA. Enough of this snarling. Get out of here, all of you. I want some rest.

THE OLD ONE. But how about The Rich One? Aren't we going to kill him?

ADELITA. Oh, no!

THE OLD ONE (*the plate in her hand, she faces* ADELITA). Why don't you weep for your pretty golden lover?

THE BLOND ONE (*sharply*). Shut your mouth on the outside of your teeth!

(*All of the women but* CONCHA *and* ADELITA *freeze into silence.* MARIA, *who has raised her gun, quietly drops it.*)

CONCHA (*looks at all of them, her eyes darting suspiciously from person to person, then she relaxes slightly*). Do I have to speak twice to you carrion crows?
(*As though a magic wand had brought them back to life again, the women relax and start moving about.* ADELITA *takes the plate from* THE OLD ONE *and hands it to* CONCHA.)

CONCHA. Thank you, Adelita. The rest of you get out of here.

THE OLD ONE (*sullenly*). But we cannot keep The Rich One much longer. He eats more than we do.

CONCHA. You can come back after a while. We'll talk about it then. Cricket!
(*The women start out.*)

CRICKET (*turning back*). What do you want?

CONCHA (*eating*). Your soldier told me to tell you that if you went again to the saloon in Saltillo he would nail your face to its door.

CRICKET (*startled*). How did he know I'd been there?

CONCHA. Knowing you, he probably guessed it. It wouldn't be hard.

CRICKET. But I only went down to Saltillo to find a mirror for our Rich beauty. What harm was there in slipping into the saloon for a minute?

CONCHA. At how many men did you roll the eye?

CRICKET. A woman has to have some fun. That soldier of mine isn't wasting his minutes, I can tell you. I've got as many rights as he has.

CONCHA. Were they Federal soldiers, or our men?

CRICKET. I don't remember. But they had gold, and they knew how to spend it.

CONCHA (*stares at her, her mouth curling*). So you don't remember. For a two-peso gold-piece you would forget the road to heaven. Get out!

CRICKET (*shrugs her shoulders as she passes* ADELITA). Perhaps The Rich One is awake now and my hand is as soft to hold as yours.
(ADELITA *draws away from her, and* CRICKET *laughs as she goes out. This by-play has not been lost on* CONCHA *who pretends that she has noticed nothing, and speaks lightly.*)

CONCHA. Thank the Saints, Adelita, you don't snarl. (*She smiles up at the girl.*) I have a message for you, too.

ADELITA (*with the interest of a child*). What kind of a message?

CONCHA (*handing* ADELITA *her plate*). From the young Rubén. He wants to know if you still love him. (MARIA *is standing at the high left end of the rock and takes no notice of this conversation.*)

ADELITA (*sniffs*). He has been gone a month and not one letter from him. I don't call that love.

CONCHA (*laughs and sings teasingly*).

So farewell my beloved Adelita,
So farewell to all that I hold most dear.
Do not sigh if I write you no letter,
I'll not change you for any girl here.

(ADELITA *squats down beside her, and* CONCHA *brushes the girl's hair back.*)

CONCHA. Anyway, you couldn't read it if he sent you one.

ADELITA (*proudly*). I can now. See, I can write my name. (*She writes it in the air as she pronounces the syllables, A . . . de . . . li . . . ta! As she crosses the "t" and dots the "i," she laughs up at* CONCHA.)

CONCHA (*with mock surprise*). Who taught you such magic?

ADELITA (*gestures with her thumb*). He did. He said that in the towns all the girls know how to read and write.

CONCHA (*suspiciously*). What else has he told you?

ADELITA. Oh, he uses a lot of words. I don't know what they mean, but they sound so beautiful. He said I made him think of red wine in an amber glass. What is amber?

CONCHA. I don't know. (*Narrows her eyes.*) So he talks about you a lot, does he?

ADELITA. Ay, yes. He says I'm the symbol of the Revolution. What is a symbol?

CONCHA. Why... it means when people look at you they think of the Revolution. What made him say that?

ADELITA. It was my name. He says that when all the soldiers sing the verses of my name, they think of me. (*She laughs.*) But that is foolish. I don't know all the soldiers.

CONCHA. He seems to be a very clever young man. I think I had better have a little talk with this Rich One.

ADELITA. But he isn't like all the other Rich Ones.

CONCHA (*raising her brows*). No? Imagine that. Did he tell you that, too?

ADELITA. Oh, yes. He says he believes in the Revolution. He wants to know all about us... everything we do, and everything Hilario does...

CONCHA. Fancy! All about us. (*Bending toward* ADELITA.) And you tell him?

Adelita. Of course I tell him. I told him a lot about you, too. He thought you were very brave to take the ammunition all alone to Hilario. He seemed surprised that Hilario would let you go back and forth all alone.

Concha (*looking over her shoulder to the right. Her sarcasm is lost on the girl*). I suppose that he was surprised when I arrived back here this morning all alone, too. Very much surprised.

Adelita (*laughs gaily*). You should have seen his face when I told him about all the ammunition we keep hidden in that cave over there, and especially about the bombs.

Concha (*laughing without mirth*). Yes, I imagine that was funny, Adelita. He sounds very amusing indeed. Do you think that he could make me laugh?

Adelita. He could make even a sad fox laugh.

Concha. Then you run and get him. But don't run back with him until I call you. I must talk to María first. (*Her mood shows irritation.*) I leave this camp for a few days, and when I come back everything is wrong. You're no better than children.

(Adelita *laughs and runs out right. The moment she is gone,* Concha's *air of light good humor is lost and she is again a worried woman. She hesitates a moment, looks up at* Maria, *then making up her mind she goes half-way up the path and calls.*)

Concha. María!

MARIA (*turns and moves toward her*). What do you want, Concha?

CONCHA. There are Federal soldiers in the mountains. (*At* MARIA's *surprise, she shrugs her shoulders.*) They almost caught me two days ago. I've had to dodge around them like a rabbit. From the way they acted anyone would think they knew I'd been to Hilario.

MARIA (*intently*). How could that be? No one here would tell them but The Rich One and we've kept our eyes on him I can tell you.

CONCHA (*doubtfully*). Cricket might have told them when she was in that saloon in Saltillo. For a handful of gold Cricket would sell her own right arm.

MARIA. If she had told them anything, she would have been afraid to come back. She hasn't the courage of a flea.

CONCHA (*turns jerkily away and folds her arms*). I know it. It's The Rich One who told them if anyone did. But how? He's a thin cord,* that one. If he is sending messages to the Federals, I must find out how he does it.

MARIA. Why worry about it, Concha? The Federals will never find this hiding place.

CONCHA. If he sent them a message about me, he can tell them how to find the way here.

MARIA (*thoughtfully*). How many Federals were there?

---

* *Thin cord* is a typical Mexican phrase which is the equivalent of "city slicker" in English.

CONCHA. It was a scouting party . . . just five or six. I don't think they were able to follow me. (*She turns and comes down to the fire.* MARIA *follows her a short distance.*) But I don't know. (*She faces* MARIA.) If they do come here . . . if they find this ammunition . . .

MARIA. It will be the end of Hilario . . . yes, I know. (*Sharply.*) If the Federals know about this place, they'd know how important this ammunition is to us. They'd send a company to get it, not just a scouting party.

CONCHA. If they know that much, they know only women are guarding it. (*With bitter humor.*) And the Federals are clever. Surely only five or six men are needed to deal with women.
(*Both the women laugh, but without mirth.*)

MARIA (*pats her gun*). I'd like to stand them up in front of me like *mescal* bottles and practice shooting their ears off.

CONCHA. You could practice on The Rich One if I knew he told them . . . or . . .

MARIA. Or what?

CONCHA (*starts pacing up and down*). Oh, I don't want to believe that Cricket had anything to do with this. If I could only be sure!

MARIA. You could find out. (*As* CONCHA *looks up at her . . . startled.*) There's more than one way of getting straw into a barn.

CONCHA (*rubbing her mouth*). Yes, I could find out, couldn't I, María? There are times when you are almost as clever as I am. (*They smile at each other, then* CONCHA *is again businesslike.*) But first of all I must find out about these Federals. Are they hunting the ammunition... or... me?

MARIA. It would be a grand thing for them if they could capture the great Concha.

CONCHA. They would shoot me dead before I could blow my nose. They would shoot any of us... even the little Adelita.

MARIA. You are the only one of us whose face is known.

CONCHA (*snaps her fingers*). Precisely. That is why I want you to do something for me. (*Looks over her shoulders toward the right, then goes up to* MARIA *and drops her hands on the woman's shoulders.*) You are a brave woman, María.

MARIA (*quietly*). What do you want me to do?

CONCHA (*very quietly*). Pretend that you are hunting for firewood. If they ask you about us...

MARIA. I will tell them nothing.

CONCHA. You will tell them the truth.

MARIA (*startled*). But then they will come here. They will take Hilario's ammunition and us, too. And what will Hilario do then?

CONCHA. Hilario will not miss one bomb, especially if it blows six Federals to hell, the wealthy ... (*She turns her head and spits.*)

MARIA. They're not easy to trap I can tell you. They've got brains...

CONCHA. Leave all that to me. You're just the bait. They'll follow you all right. They'll trust you. They'll have to trust you. But at the foot of the trail you dodge into the rocks and lose them. I don't want you between us and the Federals when we throw the bomb at them.

MARIA (*grasping* CONCHA's *arms*). Who will throw the bomb?

CONCHA. What is that to you?

MARIA. Whoever does will blow to hell with them. We're in the mountains, Concha. It will start a landslide. There wouldn't be a chance of escape...

CONCHA. Better one woman in hell than to lose Hilario's ammunition.

MARIA. I know what you're thinking. But you mustn't do it, Concha. Not you. We need you... Hilario needs you. He hasn't anybody to trust but you...

CONCHA. Don't be a fool, María.

MARIA. Give me the bomb now. When the moment comes, I'll throw it. There isn't so much danger in the valley. I might escape, and if I don't... (*She shrugs.*) I'm not much use. A woman with a dead heart never is.

CONCHA (*puts her hands on* MARIA's *shoulders, then kisses her on both cheeks*). A beautiful plan, María, but not a good one. I have to find out who is sending those messages, you see. And the only way to do it is to trick him . . . or her . . . into warning them. Now go, and may God walk with you.

MARIA. Promise me first that you won't throw it. Please, Concha.

CONCHA (*smiles gently*). I will choose when the time comes. Good-by, my friend.
(*They look at each other, then kiss each other on both cheeks and shake hands. Handing* CONCHA *her gun,* MARIA *turns and walks quickly up the path to disappear down the mountainside.* CONCHA *stares after her, then waves her arm at her. Finally she turns and comes down the path to the fire. She looks down at it, then, with grief almost too great for her to bear, she crosses her wrists above her head and her body droops forward. In a moment she straightens, goes up right, and calls softly.*)

CONCHA. Cricket! Cricket! Come here. (*She returns to the fire and squats down as* CRICKET *enters.*)

CRICKET (*half to* CONCHA, *half to herself*). That Tomasa and The Old One! All they can talk about is their sons. What's a poor woman who never had a son going to say? The only thing that ever happened to me was when the Rich Ones carried me off on my fourteenth saint's day. They brought me back quick enough, I can tell you. (*She sighs.*) One of them used soap that smelt like violets. Every time I smell a violet now I can remember the feel of my knife going into his stomach. Oh, well, the poor sinner's getting more rest than I am ... be damned to him!

CONCHA. Stop your grumbling and get up there on the path. Take María's gun and hide behind that rock. If you stick your head up before I call you, I'll shoot it out between your ears.

CRICKET (*whining*). I hear you.

(*She hides behind the rock on the path. Not until she is hidden does* CONCHA call.)

CONCHA. Adelita! You can bring in The Rich One now. (*There is a brief pause, then* ADELITA *can be heard laughing off right. In a moment she enters with* THE RICH ONE *whose left arm is in a sling made of a red bandanna handkerchief. He walks with a bravado air as though he would show the world how brave he is.*)

ADELITA. Here he is, Concha.

CONCHA (*without raising her head*). Do not try to escape, Rich One. I have only to raise my voice and my women will shoot you before you run two feet. Come around here where I can get a look at you.

THE RICH ONE (*shrugs and comes down to her*). You said you had seen enough of my dirty face the day you captured me.

CONCHA (*raising her head*). I never look at Rich Ones unless I have to. What happened to your arm?

The Rich One. One of your mosquitoes stung me this morning.

Concha (*stands*). If they have been sticking cactus thorns into you...

The Rich One (*holds up his head*). They did not like the direction in which I was running.

Concha. Oh, so you tried to escape? (*Walks up to him.*) You do not like us, perhaps?

The Rich One. As individuals, señora, you are magnificent... but in a crowd? (*He bows slightly.*) Forgive me, señora.

Adelita (*proudly*). Didn't I tell you he used big words? And, oh, you should hear him sing. Sing the *ADELITA* for Concha.

The Rich One (*shrugs and turns away*). With my poor voice, I am afraid...

Concha. What is the matter? Are you afraid of the mountain air?

The Rich One (*meaningly*). On the contrary. I find that it gives me a zest... for life.

Concha. Really? And this new joy does not make you want to break out into song?

The Rich One. I prefer not to sing.

CONCHA. You hear, Adelita? I am afraid our fine gentleman is too proud to sing for us. After all, if there were no Revolution, perhaps we should be his servants.

THE RICH ONE (*looking insolently at* CONCHA). I am glad the señora realizes that even the Revolution does not change . . . blood.

CONCHA (*walks up to him, her head very high*). Precisely. Pigs remain pigs. You will sing for us.

THE RICH ONE (*coldly*). But I do not care to . . .

CONCHA (*harshly*). I said that you will sing. Sit down, Adelita, while the . . . gentleman . . . gets his breath. (*Both the women sit down.*)

THE RICH ONE (*looking at* CONCHA *for a moment as though he would like to kill her, he smiles sarcastically and bows*). Always at your service, señora. (*He quite obviously sings to* ADELITA.)

And Adelita's the name of my loved one,
She's the girl whom I never shall forget.
In the world I have found a fair flower,
I remember the night we first met.

If Adelita would say she would wed me,
If Adelita would only be my wife,
I would buy her a fine dress of satin,
She could wear it the rest of her life.

CONCHA (*flings up her arm*). Stop! You have no heart! What do you know of the song of the Revolution? It has fire! It has life!

Scene from SOLDADERA

THE RICH ONE: But you are magnificent, senora.

(*She flings back her head and sings it for him. The magnetism, the vitality of this woman attracts* THE RICH ONE *so that for a moment he loses his air of superiority.*)

I'm a soldier and now I must leave you,
For my country has called on me to fight.
Adelita, Adelita, my loved one,
You must not, dear, forget me tonight.

So farewell once again, Adelita,
So farewell to all your grace and all your
charms,
Now I go with the hope of returning,
To come back once more to your arms.

(*As* CONCHA *finishes singing she faces him triumphantly.*)

THE RICH ONE (*with enthusiasm*). But you are magnificent, señora!

CONCHA (*turns away*). Thank you. And now . . . leave us, Adelita.

ADELITA (*plaintively*). But, Concha . . .

CONCHA (*almost sharply*). Leave us, child.
(ADELITA *looks at both of them curiously, and then walks out right. Both* CONCHA *and* THE RICH ONE *look after her until she is gone, then he moves toward* CONCHA. *It is obvious that this woman attracts him, doubtless because he has never seen anyone quite like*

her before in his life. The face she turns toward him, however, is so bitter and cold that it stops his forward movement.)

CONCHA. We might as well do this the right way, not that I love talking. But if Hilario asks me questions, I have to answer him, don't I?

THE RICH ONE (*looking at her intently, but his voice is once more sarcastic*). You know him better than I do, señora.

CONCHA (*harshly*). I don't want any sneers from you. And take off your hat. I'm no common soldier's woman.

THE RICH ONE (*taking off his hat and bowing*). Great ladies have always frightened me. You will have to excuse my poor manners.

CONCHA (*seeming to grow nervous under his scrutiny*). You won't need manners where you're going. But one thing at a time. What's your name?

THE RICH ONE. Will I need that where I'm going?

CONCHA. I asked you a question. Answer it.

THE RICH ONE. For what it's worth to you, my name is Mario Galicia. I'm a lawyer by profession.

CONCHA. And what is a lawyer doing in these mountains?

THE RICH ONE. I'd been in Saltillo. Although I'm a Torreón man myself, there aren't many mountains in that direction. I thought I'd look at one close to while I had the chance.

CONCHA (*thinks this over, then glances sideways at him*). What do they raise around Torreón?

THE RICH ONE (*smiles with assurance*). Wheat.

CONCHA. That's right. What else do they raise?

THE RICH ONE (*no longer smiling*). Why... oranges.

CONCHA (*easily*). That's a lie. They raise cotton. What's the biggest factory?

THE RICH ONE (*breathing quickly*). Soap.

CONCHA. Excellent. And what is the name of the factory?

THE RICH ONE. Señora, I object...

CONCHA (*smoothly*). What is the name of the factory?

THE RICH ONE (*turns away slightly, then to her triumphantly*). The Mariposa.

CONCHA. That's the name of a brand of soap.

THE RICH ONE (*angrily*). I'm a lawyer, not a dealer in soap. How should I know what the name of their factory is?

CONCHA. I thought perhaps your office might be close to it.

THE RICH ONE. A distance I believe of two blocks. Perhaps three. I don't know. What is the difference?

CONCHA. Hilario likes to know these little details. Now let me be sure that I have the details correct. Your name is Mario Galicia, you are a lawyer, and your office is two blocks from the famous soap factory in the city of Torreón.

THE RICH ONE (*easily*). Precisely.

CONCHA (*looking at him thoughtfully*). You know, I have a feeling that Hilario isn't going to believe that.

THE RICH ONE. Why not?

CONCHA. Well, Hilario used to work in that factory and those two blocks must be awfully long blocks.

THE RICH ONE. What do you mean?

CONCHA. Nothing. Only the soap factory is in the town of Gomez Palacio in the state of Durango, while Torreón is in the state of Coahuila...three miles away. What part of the south are you from? I want the truth now.

THE RICH ONE (*sullenly*). Cuernavaca.

CONCHA. And you had to come up here to see a mountain, eh? All the way from Cuernavaca that's 1,500 meters above the sea. Pah! We of the north know more about the south than you southerners know about us. And the next time you pretend to come from Torreón, use a Torreón accent. If there is a next time.

The Rich One (*sharply*). What do you care where I come from, or why I came? I'm here and you're going to shoot me, and that's the end of it.

Concha (*laughing softly*). Shoot you? Yes, we *could* shoot you.

The Rich One. I don't see what all this talk amounts to anyway. They promised me a fine execution when you got back. Well, you're here.

Concha. This killing doesn't seem to worry you.

The Rich One. Would my weeping make you more merciful?

Concha. It might give us all a good laugh.

The Rich One (*starts to light a cigarette, remembers his manners and offers one to* Concha). Do you want a cigarette?

Concha (*startled at this unusual courtesy*). Why... thank you. (*As she takes one.*) Of course you understand I've not got anything against you myself.

The Rich One (*as he lights her cigarette*). Yes, I realize that. But for a man... to die is easy.

Concha (*blowing out a puff of smoke*). Is it?

THE RICH ONE (*stares at her*). Why not? A bullet through the heart, blackness, and then . . . (*He blows out the match.*)

CONCHA. Precisely. If we shoot you, but we won't. (*She explains the situation as though she slightly regretted it, as between adults, but what can you do with children who get out of control?*) It's Tomasa and The Old One. They've suffered a lot from your kind, and Hilario never would let them play with any of his prisoners, so they've been looking forward to you.

THE RICH ONE (*to whom this idea is very new*). You mean . . . you mean they want to torture me?

CONCHA. Why not?

THE RICH ONE. But you are women . . . not hardened soldiers.

CONCHA (*more to herself than to him*). Are we women? Sometimes I wonder. The Old One who cooks our food . . . she saw her son crucified by men of your kind . . . another one saw her son hunted down by dogs for the sport of it. That doesn't make women, my friend. That makes something worse than the devils in hell.

THE RICH ONE. But I had nothing to do with their sorrows. Why do they want to torture me?

CONCHA. You called Adelita a symbol of the Revolution. Well, you're a symbol to us. You're a symbol of all the hate and horror that the Rich Ones have made for us. There are no men here to tell us what to do. We stand alone. You are merely the victim. That is not our fault.

THE RICH ONE (*looking down at his clenched hand*). You do not seem very anxious for me to die. You've kept me alive five days.

CONCHA. We wanted you to look forward to dying. We wanted you to wake up each morning and think, "This is the last time I shall ever see the dawn... the last time I shall ever hear a bird sing... the last time I shall ever feel the heat of the sun."

THE RICH ONE (*laughing harshly to cover a growing fear*). Señora, I am not a sentimentalist. My thoughts were quite different, I assure you.

CONCHA. Yes, I know they were, but the women didn't know that. I saw no reason to keep them from enjoying your agony.

THE RICH ONE. You are very wise. Perhaps you know what I was thinking.

CONCHA (*softly*). Perhaps I do. Perhaps you were thinking, "Today the Federals will be here. Today they will come and save me and capture all this ammunition." Do you think I don't know a spy when I see one? Aye! Your face of ashes stinks like rotten meat.

THE RICH ONE (*blustering*). So now I am a spy. What a magnificent imagination you have. I let you capture me, I suppose, and then I send messages out to the Federals to tell them what you are doing. I am guarded night and day but still I find a means to send messages. Señora, I am no fool!

CONCHA (*gravely*). That's the trouble. For once you are too smart for me. I don't know how you send the messages... (*She looks up toward the rock where* CRICKET *is hiding, then back at him.*) ... but you send them just the same.

THE RICH ONE. Since you are so clever, señora... suppose you work your brain over that, too.

CONCHA. Adelita had something to do with it. You weren't wasting all that fine talk on her for nothing. First you found out everything you wanted to know from her, the innocent child.

THE RICH ONE. Perhaps I got her to carry my messages for me... (*Pauses and adds climactically.*) ... if I sent them. You see, I admit nothing.

CONCHA. But Adelita isn't foolish enough to carry news from you to the Federals. No, you used her... or someone... in a way without her knowing it, but how? (THE RICH ONE *laughs.*) You needn't laugh. I'll find out.

THE RICH ONE (*sneering*). I suppose you women think you can stop the Federals, now you know so well they are coming.

CONCHA. I'll stop them, never fear. They'll be making a nice warm nest for you on the tail of Grandfather Devil.

THE RICH ONE. It has been five days. You are too late to stop them now.

CONCHA (*tossing away her cigarette*). Then you admit that you are a spy?

THE RICH ONE (*flings out his hand. The sense of the Federals' nearness has overcome his fear of these women*). Why not? They are too close now for you to go running to Hilario for help. And if you shot me down here and now, what good would it do? The Federals might make it easier on you if you had a live prisoner to give them. They know I'm here. They'll hunt for me. My dead body won't help you any.

CONCHA. Are you trying to make a bargain with me?

THE RICH ONE. You're smarter than those other women. Come over to the Federals while I'm giving you the chance. (*Walks closer to her.*) I like you. I'm no small change with the Federals, I can tell you. Those soldiers will do as I say.

CONCHA. And if I say no?

THE RICH ONE (*puts his unwounded hand around her throat*). My fingers are strong. I have only to press a little, and there would be no voice left in your throat to call for help. I would be up the path and away before your women could reach you. And then it would be too late.

CONCHA (*as his fingers start to close she calls faintly in a strangled voice*). Cricket!

CRICKET (*straightens behind the rocks and points her gun at* THE RICH ONE). Drop your hand.

THE RICH ONE (*swings around and stares up at* CRICKET, *then turns back to* CONCHA *and speaks with honest admiration*). You are worth two generals, señora.

CONCHA (*looks at him and smiles faintly, then goes to the base of the rock on which* CRICKET *is standing*). Did you hear what we said, Cricket?

CRICKET. Every word.

CONCHA. What do you think?

CRICKET (*looking cautiously at her*). I don't know. What do you think, Concha?

CONCHA (*laughs*). Always the cautious one, our Cricket. She jumps out of danger as easily as her namesake.

THE RICH ONE. It's the Federals who have the money.

CONCHA. Good clothes again...good food. The way it used to be.

THE RICH ONE. The little things that women like. Perfume, jewelry, holy medals like this one. (*He pulls the medal that dangles on a cord about his neck out of his shirt and shows it to her.*)

CONCHA (*touching it lightly, then bending forward to kiss it*). To go to Church again. I haven't been to Church in almost a year.

THE RICH ONE. The safety of a sheltered life. The Federals can give you safety.

CONCHA (*shakes her head*). I don't know. Hilario has given me excitement...danger. I love danger. A sheltered life doesn't mean very much any more.

THE RICH ONE. But think of how amusing it would be ...learning to live all over again.

CONCHA. I...I don't know what to say.

CRICKET (*still watching* CONCHA). What has happened to you, Concha? I never saw you sway back and forth before...like a straw in the wind.

CONCHA. What if I tell you I'm sick of all this...of the dirt and the filth, of sleeping on the ground in rain and cold? ...

CRICKET (*puzzled at this new* CONCHA). But what about Hilario?

CONCHA. Yes, and I'm sick of him, too. Every peso he gets he spends on ammunition.

THE RICH ONE. The Federals know how to spend their money on women.

CRICKET. I saw one of their generals down at the saloon the other night. He was plastered all over with gold like a statue in the Church...

THE RICH ONE. This Revolution can't last. Your men are good men, but they need money. And they don't know how to fight. They waste their energy chasing around all over the map trying to keep out of our way. And after the fighting is all over what have you got left but some burned-down houses, and some black clothes for mourning?

CRICKET. He's right, Concha. It's the Federals you see spending money in the saloons. And what have we got against the Rich Ones . . . you and me?

CONCHA. Years ago on the great ranch when my father was foreman for old Don Ramón, there used to be dances and flowers and music. Then Don Ramón died, and the ranch was sold, and the new owner came. I was young and pretty then. (*She looks up at* THE RICH ONE.) Would you think I had ever been young and pretty? (THE RICH ONE *smiles and kisses her hand, but she draws her hand away, seeming not to notice the gesture.*) The new owner thought so. He shot my father when he tried to . . . when he tried to protect me . . .

CRICKET (*interrupting what to her is a very boring recital*). But now his soul's in paradise with the Blessed Angels. He won't be burning in hell like you and me.

CONCHA. I don't know. I don't know what to do. Hilario has been good to me. He trusts me, and so do the women.

CRICKET. Tomasa and The Old One would groan and complain whichever side they were on. They're too old to be living anyway. But you and me, we could find plenty of rich soldiers. There was one Federal with a gold watch, and the prettiest black mustaches.

THE RICH ONE. There's plenty of Federal soldiers who would give three gold watches to slip his arm around Concha's waist.

CONCHA (*laughs sharply*). Three gold watches.

THE RICH ONE. Perhaps four. And plenty of *tequila** to drink. No cheap *mescal* for them.

CONCHA (*almost hysterically*). All right, I'll do it. Let them take Hilario's ammunition. What do I care? I'm tired of this Revolution. I'm tired of fighting. I want to sing again, and dance again... dance!
(THE RICH ONE *with a triumphant laugh puts his good arm around her waist and they swing in gay circles while* CRICKET *claps her hands; but abruptly* THE RICH ONE *lets go of* CONCHA *and catches his wounded shoulder.* CONCHA *half supports him.*)

THE RICH ONE. I'm all right. If your women make love as well as they dance and shoot... (*His light tone ends in a gasp of pain.*)

CONCHA. I forgot. (*She glances right, cautious again.*) The women will be suspicious if we are not careful. I'll have to stall them off. We can't do this too suddenly. We can't have them suspecting anything or they'll blow us all up, too.

THE RICH ONE. I knew you'd see the right thing to do.

---

* *Tequila:* This is a refined *mescal.*

CONCHA. We'll have to hold a trial to see which way we are going to kill you, Rich One. (*As he draws back, she adds persuasively.*) That's the only way I can make time. And you, Cricket, you think up just as good ideas as they have. They mustn't suspect anything.

CRICKET (*still delighted at the idea of future wealth*). You can trust me.

THE RICH ONE. When the Federals arrive, you let me handle them.

CONCHA. Why not? You know them better than I do. (*Puts her hand on his arm.*) You are sure that they will come, aren't you? I won't feel safe until I know that they are climbing that mountain.

THE RICH ONE. Don't worry. They're coming.

CONCHA. Perhaps... you should send them another message.

THE RICH ONE. I sent them one this morning. (*He looks up at the sun.*) They should be here in... in another hour.

CONCHA. You know, you have courage. I don't think I could have waited as patiently for certain death as you have.

THE RICH ONE. That's the beautiful joke. I knew the Federals were going to save me. There was nothing to be brave about.

CONCHA (*looks at him a moment in contempt*). I see. (*Jerks her head up and looks at* CRICKET.) Call the women, Cricket.
(CRICKET *goes to the edge of the rock, claps her hands together twice, then beckons with her arm.*)

CONCHA (*to* THE RICH ONE). There's only one thing. Keep Adelita away from them.

THE RICH ONE. Don't let that worry you. She's mine. I picked her out the minute I saw her.

CONCHA (*hard for a moment*). Did you? (*Instantly gay again.*) Now remember, Rich One, whatever happens don't get nervous. (*She goes down to the fire, as* THE OLD ONE *enters.*)

THE OLD ONE (*muttering*). So much talking when we could be killing him.

CONCHA. Bring me a bottle of *mescal.*

THE OLD ONE. Always wanting something new. Never wanting what you've got. (*Goes into the cave left.*)

CONCHA. You heard me! Get a move on you.

TOMASA (*talking to* THE BLOND ONE *as they enter*). I say the ants are better than a *maguey* * plant.

---

* *Maguey:* Type of cactus found extensively in Mexico. Grows exceedingly fast—three feet in a night. The sap of the *maguey* is used as an inebriating drink, called *mescal.*

THE BLOND ONE. There aren't enough ants around here.

TOMASA (*pulling a small bottle out of a pocket in her skirt*). I've been catching them. I've got enough in here to eat him, and they're hungry, the little darlings!

THE OLD ONE (*who has entered with a bottle of* mescal, *and hands it to* CONCHA). Here you are. I've had to hide it in the box of bombs to keep it from these crows.

CONCHA. Salt and lemon, you old fool.

THE OLD ONE (*behind the fire*). I'm getting them . . . I'm getting them.

TOMASA (*inspecting* THE RICH ONE *as though he were a piece of dried beef*). A little honey on the eyelids and under his armpits and these little babies will soon make some pretty holes in him. They're nice large red ants. (*As* THE RICH ONE, *a little sick, shuts his eyes and turns his face away from her.*) Look at him, shaking already. He'll be screaming by tomorrow morning, like my son did when the dogs were after him, bless his sweet soul in heaven!

CONCHA (*takes lemon and salt from* THE OLD ONE. *Pours a little salt in the palm of her hand, then runs the cut lemon across her tongue, takes a drink from the bottle, and finishes by licking the salt from her palm.* She spits to one side*). Where is Adelita?

ADELITA (*coming forward out of the shadows to the right*). Here I am, Concha.

---

* This is the traditional Mexican method of drinking *mescal.*

CONCHA. Stand here beside me. (*She looks at the women who are spread out in front of the mouth of the cave, all but* CRICKET, *who is on the sentry rock.*) Women, we have to do with the death of a Rich One.
(*There is a general unrest here, not so much of nervousness as hidden excitement.*)

CRICKET (*enjoying this*). May he roast in the devil's own mouth!

CONCHA. Silence! You, Cricket, watch the trail for María. The moment you see her coming, tell me.
(*This startles* THE RICH ONE. *He looks up at* CRICKET *then at* CONCHA *and then back to* CRICKET *again. He knows that these women are no more to be trusted than mad dogs.*)

CRICKET. I have as much right to say how he will die as any of the rest of you. After all, I saw him first.

THE BLOND ONE. Look out, Cricket. Somebody will win the lottery ahead of you.
(*She,* TOMASA, *and* THE OLD ONE *laugh loudly.*)

CONCHA (*sharply*). You heard me. Watch the trail.

CRICKET. When the time comes, may I tie him up?

CONCHA. Yes, if you want to.

CRICKET (*to* THE BLOND ONE). Chew that in your gullet, you blond daughter of a sea-sick spider.

CONCHA (*as* THE BLOND ONE *snatches up a stone to throw at* CRICKET). To your place, you blond fool! (CRICKET *laughs and disappears up the trail.*) Now remember, you will talk one at a time as I call your names. And the first two that get into a fight I will beat until they can't stand up. You, first, Old One.

THE OLD ONE (*moves to center*). I say nail him to a tree, like his kind nailed my boy, and then let me slit his stomach from side to side...

CONCHA. Remember that, Adelita. (*Turns her face slightly toward* THE RICH ONE.) One, to crucify him. –Oh, Rich One, you may sit down.

THE RICH ONE (*who is beginning to grow more nervous*). Thank you, señora. (*He sits down, all the women staring at him.*)

CONCHA. And now you, Blondie.

THE BLOND ONE. I say the cactus plant. We have lots of *maguey* around here. They grow three feet in the night if you put a little water in the roots. Why the sharp point will grow right through that nervous, white heart of his.*

CONCHA. Adelita, the second is the *maguey* plant.

(ADELITA *is drawing slowly away from the circle toward* THE RICH ONE.)

* Death by *maguey* was a common mode of execution during the Revolution. The prisoner would be spread-eagled above the plant, and his body would be left as an example to the enemy.

TOMASA. It's my time to speak and I say the ants, the red ants eating through his flesh. I have them right here waiting for him...hungry for him, the little darlings. (*Flourishes her bottle.*)

CONCHA. And the third, Adelita, is the little red ant.

THE OLD ONE. What do you say, Concha?

CONCHA. I am the judge here, and my thoughts do not matter.

THE BLOND ONE. We've all spoken, haven't we? Which way do we finish him off?
(THE RICH ONE, *his eyes fastened on* CONCHA, *half rises to his feet, then sinks back down again, slipping* CRICKET's *mirror from his pocket. He runs his hand over it again and again as though trying to shine its surface, while pretending to shape his mustache.*)

CONCHA. Adelita hasn't spoken.

THE BLOND ONE. What does the baby say about her pretty Rich One?

ADELITA (*moving forward*). I say you are animals, all of you...worse than animals. All you can think of are terrible things...things you shouldn't think about... devil's things!

TOMASA (*whining*). You shut her up, Concha. She's got no right to talk like that.

CONCHA. She's got as much right as any of the rest of us. Leave her alone. I want to hear what she has to say.

ADELITA. You are making something ugly and horrible out of the Revolution. And it isn't ugly... it's beautiful! What if the Rich Ones did kill your son, Tomasa? Will killing him bring your son back to life? Will the wrong they did to your son, you Old One, be made right if you do the same to him? I don't know what you're all thinking about. It isn't human... it isn't the Tomasa and the Blondie and the Old One and the Concha that I have always known. And Cricket up there looking forward to tying him up! Oh, you are horrible, horrible!

THE BLOND ONE. You don't know what you're talking about. Why shouldn't we hate him and his breed? They took my man, didn't they, and hung him from the door of his own house. And María. How about María? They made her stand and watch while they tore her man's eyes out, didn't they? We can't do anything to them that's worse than what they've done to us! We're human, aren't we?

ADELITA. But that's over... that's finished. Nothing we do now can change that. Because they were brutes and animals, does that make us brutes and animals, too?

CONCHA. Adelita! Come here, child.

ADELITA. I don't want to touch you. I don't want to touch any of you. You're not the women I used to know... you're not the women who used to carry me around on your backs when my mother died. You've changed, all of you, horribly changed! Why, you're just like you're dead to me. All of the goodness and sweetness that used to be in you . . . it's dead! (*Crouches on the ground, crying bitterly.*)

TOMASA. This is the Revolution, not a nursery.

ADELITA. What do you know about the Revolution? It's beautiful, it's glorious, it's heroic. It's giving all you've got to freedom. It's dying with the sun in your face, not being eaten to death by little red ants in a bottle. If this is your Revolution, I don't want to see it . . . I don't want to see it!

CONCHA (*standing*). Yes, this is the Revolution. We had to forget how to weep, and how to be kind and merciful. We are cruel, because the Revolution is cruel. It must crush out the evil before we can make things good again.

TOMASA. Crush it lower than the earth.

CONCHA. Adelita, Adelita, for you there is tomorrow, but for us there is only yesterday. The Revolution is a fire that flames up and destroys, and we are the fire.

THE BLOND ONE. Burning, burning, let us burn them all.

CONCHA. We are the flame, calling to flame, and we are the earth calling to earth, and we are the tempest blowing across the sky!

THE OLD ONE. Blowing us like dead leaves in the wind.

CONCHA. Your Rich One and his kind have crushed us down to ashes, but we are the spark that has kindled a new, a roaring blaze. If we have learned how to be cruel, he has taught us our lesson. Look at him sitting there, winking at his face in a mirror, Adelita, and we with his death in our hands!

CRICKET (*running down the path*). I see María coming. She's almost at the top of the trail! And below her are men in uniform crawling up the mountain. (*She sees* THE RICH ONE *who is standing now, and quite openly trying to make the sun reflect from his mirror.*) Ay, The Rich One is flirting with the sun again. And what pretty words is he telling you today?

TOMASA. Is he telling you that tomorrow you will be ant's meat? Is that what he has been telling you all the week long?

CONCHA (*slowly*). A mirror and the sun. A mirror to shine in the sun! (*Snatches it from him.*) So that is how you talked to your friends!

THE RICH ONE (*catching her wrist*). Silence, you fool. Do you want to spoil everything?

CONCHA. Blondie, bring me...

BLONDIE. I can guess what you want. (*She runs into the cave, left.*)

ADELITA. What are you going to do?

CONCHA. I am going to catch some rabbits and use the Rich One for bait!

MARIA (*running in, down the path*). I got away from them at the foot of the path but they are already climbing it. There are five of them.

CONCHA (*freeing her wrist*). And this one makes six.

THE RICH ONE. So you thought you would trick me, eh? Well, trick plays to trick. Listen to me, women. She was going to sell you out... sell you out to me for the price of three gold watches.

TOMASA. As though we would believe your lying tongue.

THE RICH ONE (*runs up the path to* CRICKET). If you don't believe me, ask the Cricket here.

CRICKET (*frightened*). I don't know anything. I don't know what he's talking about.

THE RICH ONE. How about the Federal general you wanted... the one plastered over with gold... like an image in the Church?

CRICKET (*haltingly*). He's making it up. Out of his head, he's making it up.

THE RICH ONE. You're not women, any of you. You're vultures... flying around to see what dead bodies you can pick on.

THE BLOND ONE (*entering from the cave with a bomb in her hands*). Here's the bomb,* Concha.

---

* During the Revolution bombs were made of bottles filled with explosives.

CONCHA (*not looking at her*). Light the fuse.

THE RICH ONE (*screams*). You're not going to blow me to hell with your bombs.
(*He tries to run up the path but* TOMASA *and* THE OLD ONE *catch his arms, one on either side. As* TOMASA *drops to her knees, her weight on his wounded arm makes him stop struggling and he drops his head, biting his lips with pain.*)

THE BLOND ONE (*who has been lighting the long fuse with a twig from the fire*). Here is the bomb. (*Hands it to* CONCHA.)

MARIA. You mustn't throw it, Concha. Not you.

TOMASA (*holding out one arm, the other arm still clutching* THE RICH ONE). You belong to us, Concha. We need you. Not you!

MARIA (*running down the path to* CONCHA). What will we do without you? You belong to us!

CONCHA (*laughs sharply*). You throw it, Cricket. You love the Rich Ones and their gold braid.

CRICKET (*screams*). No! Not me! (*Runs down, flings herself on her knees and throws both arms about* CONCHA's *knees.*) I wouldn't have a chance in a landslide. I don't want to die. Not me! I was only fooling. I didn't mean what I said. Please, Concha, not me, please. I don't want to die.

CONCHA. Choose quickly, my friend. Would you rather have Tomasa's red ants eating out your eyes?
(CRICKET *screams and flings both arms up over her face.*)

ADELITA (*running toward them*). Wait. I will throw it.
(*She snatches the bomb from* CONCHA.)

CONCHA (*horrified*). No!

ADELITA (*strikes* CONCHA *with her free arm and knocks her to the ground*). This is the Revolution! The sun will be in my face!
(*She flings back her head after the triumphant cry and* THE RICH ONE, *seeing the path free, gives a desperate pull, dashes past the women, and up the path.*)

THE RICH ONE (*screaming to the Federals*). Back, you fools, back!

ADELITA (*running up the path after him*). Long live the Revolution!
(*There is a stunned silence, then* CONCHA *springs to her feet, jerking herself free from the clutching hands of* CRICKET, *and runs to the path.*)

CONCHA (*screaming*). Adelita! Adelita! (*As she reaches the great rock the sound of an explosion* * *stops her.*

---

* *Production note:* The explosion is made by firing a shotgun down a flight of stairs. The landslide is produced by a large trough filled with gravel which is tilted, slowly at first, then with increasing speed. To this is added the noise of a thunder-sheet.

She stops as though frozen, and there is a silence, followed by the awful sound of a landslide. As the echoes die away she turns dully, and looks down at the women below her.)

CONCHA. Well, she got to them in time. The ammunition is safe. Aren't you glad? Aren't you happy? Hilario can fight on for the Revolution. You should show how happy you are. You should sing. Yes, sing, you devil's vomit, *sing!*

If Adelita should go with another,
If Adelita should leave me all alone...

(*As the women slowly join in the song,* CONCHA *stops singing, and her outflung arms drop slowly to her side.*)

THE WOMEN (*singing softly*).

I would follow in a boat made of thunder,
I would follow in a train made of bone.

THE CURTAINS CLOSE

THE RED VELVET GOAT

A TRAGEDY OF LAUGHTER AND

A COMEDY OF TEARS

THE CHARACTERS

As originally produced by The Carolina Playmakers at Chapel Hill, North Carolina, on April 25, 1936.

ESTEBAN, *who longs to own a goat* . . . William Chichester
MARIANA, *his wife* . . . . Hester Barlow
LORENZO, *their son* . . . . Robert du Four
LOLA } *village girls, friends of* { Audrey Rowell
CARMEN } *Ester* . . . . } Frances Johnston
ESTER, *a village girl with whom Lorenzo is in love* . . . . Ruth Mengel
RAMON, *a peddler of women's clothing* Holman Milhous
DON PEPE, *the mayor of the village* . Gerald Hochman
DOÑA BERTA, *a neighbor and grand lady of the village* . . . . Janie Britt
OTHER VILLAGERS: Herbert Kane, Mary Delaney, Kenneth Bartlett, Jean Walker, George Starks, Conrad Poppenhusen, Thomas O'Flaherty.

THE SCENE: The patio of Esteban's house in the Street of the Arches in the town of The Three Marys, Mexico.

THE TIME: The present. Six o'clock of an afternoon in June.

THE SCENE

The late afternoon sun has thrown a golden haze over the patio of ESTEBAN'S *home. It is not a magnificent patio. There is no fountain with flowers banked around it, as in the home of* DON PEPE, *although there are pots of flowers on the stoop of the door which opens into a bedroom on the right. If it were noon, there would be chickens scratching about, and perhaps a baby pig or two, but it is evening, and the livestock have been closed up in the corral which is beyond the gate on the left.*

There are benches in front of us, and two rocking chairs swaying back and forth in front of a platform that is made of planks resting on saw-horses placed against the outside wall of the house at the back. This platform, these chairs, these benches are not usually found in ESTEBAN'S *patio, but they are here this afternoon because he is going to present a play of his own composition. The platform is in a very convenient place, since there is a door leading into the living-room which serves very well for the actors to make their entrances and exits. That funny little box in front of the platform is for the prompter, and those gray blankets dangling from the rope attached to the posts at the two front corners of the platform serve as curtains.*

To the left, now partly closed, is the great wooden door that opens directly on the street from the patio, and if you care to peer through the iron-barred window in the right wall you will see MARIANA'S *dress, which she intends to wear in her husband's play, laid out on the bed.*

The boy standing on the platform, clutching the stool in his two hands is LORENZO, *very brown of eyes and skin and very black of hair. He wears the white pyjama suit of the tropics, with a red bandanna knotted at the throat. Because he is twenty-two, old enough to have a sweetheart, he has on a pair of bright yellow shoes that frankly hurt.*

That woman standing to the right with her hands buckled on her hips, that flaming, flashing woman is MARIANA, *his mother. Although she is forty there is no gray in the black satin cap of her hair; there are no wrinkles in the smooth golden cream of her skin; and as for her body . . . well, even the loose white blouse and the billowing red muslin skirt can not hide the youthful fire in that pretty body.*

It seems almost impossible to think of ESTEBAN, *the man leaning against the edge of the platform to the left . . . it seems almost impossible to think of this funny, fat little man as being* MARIANA'S *husband. Sometimes he wakes up in the night, especially after feast days, and wonders himself how he ever came to marry such a gorgeous creature. Poor* ESTEBAN *with his funny little blob of a nose perched in the middle of a round moon face, is no match for* MARIANA *and he knows it. His hands are always aimlessly clutching at each other. They are doing it now as he watches* LORENZO *with the stool.*

MARIANA (*impatiently to* LORENZO). No, fool! Where are your brains? Remove the chair and place it in the corner to the right. Esteban, speak! You are the master of the play.

ESTEBAN. To hear you rattle on, a man would think it was your scene. (*Points left.*) The stool goes there.

MARIANA (*points right*). No, there! Would you have it hide the door?

ESTEBAN (*angrily*). I say that it goes there! Lorenzo, place it where I say or I will break your head!

LORENZO (*who, through the argument has been standing still patiently holding the stool now bangs it down in front of him on the platform*). Holy saints! Whom am I to obey? I'll put it here, and you can change it where you like. I am an actor, not a doll on strings. I must go read my part again. (*Goes out through the platform door, slamming it behind him.*)
(MARIANA *hides a laugh.*)

MARIANA. He says he is an actor. Ha! Then I am queen of tragedy. What hour does it grow to be?

ESTEBAN (*taking a large gold watch from his pocket*). My watch says eight, so then it must be six. (*Bends toward her, clasping his hands tightly together.*) Does all the world know of the benefit?

MARIANA. Musicians played before each door in town. I sent Lorenzo out with notices this morning. Do you think our guests will pay enough to buy a goat? (*Sinks down on the end of one of the benches.*)

ESTEBAN. We only need ten pesos for a goat. Don Pepe said he'd sell us one of his. With the money from its milk and cheese we'll have enough to buy another one, and soon we'll have a flock. Then we'll be the richest two in town.

MARIANA (*scornfully*). Just with one goat? What silken dreams you can build from air. To hear you speak no man in all the northern part of Mexico will be so rich as you when this play is done.

ESTEBAN (*with modest pride*). My talents are so varied, Mariana. Perhaps we should not buy a goat at all. Anyone can own a goat, but I, and I alone, can compose such drama.

MARIANA. A truth, a little truth indeed, my 'Steban. No other man could write such plays . . . (*flaring at him*) . . . because he would not write them. I think it best to buy the goat.

ESTEBAN (*shocked*). Have you no soul, no breath of genius blowing through your feeble brain? In time the world shall hear of this Esteban and mourn the fact that he possessed such a blockhead for a wife.

MARIANA (*peeved*). Who gave you hints of how to write it best but me, me, me! Who furnished you with chairs, and clothes, and men? Yes, men? (*Goes to him, her eyes burning with anger.*) Lorenzo is my son as much as yours. Oh, when I wept and cried the night that he made his first entry in the world I did not think that he would grow to be an actor.

ESTEBAN. Do not fear. My son has failed to grasp my talent. He...

MARIANA. Is better, far, than you will ever be.

ESTEBAN (*grandly ignoring her*). Did you bring the vase from Doña Berta's?

MARIANA. It is on the table in the house next to my red and blue one. You see, I do not forget, even if you do. (*Goes into the bedroom right.*)

ESTEBAN (*following her to the door and calling after her*). Now what have I forgotten?

MARIANA (*from inside*). Just a prompter, that is all. (*She enters, goes to the platform and places the vases on the prompter's box, standing back to see the effect.*) A little prompter to aid us with his book when we forget.

ESTEBAN (*with a gasp*). I meant to ask Don Pepe...

MARIANA (*sarcastically*). Did you indeed? Don Pepe, the mayor of The Three Marys! Perhaps you would prefer to have the President of the Republic, or the great civil judge to read our lines for us! Where are your wits, fool? Hanging from your nose like Spanish moss upon an ancient wind-blown tree?

ESTEBAN (*wringing his hands*). It grows near the hour of our performance! Why did you not remind me of this small detail?

MARIANA (*flings her arms above her head*). Remind you! Saints in Heaven! Holy Mary aid me! Oh, what ass is this dressed in man's clothing? Must I remember everything? Or was the play of your invention?

ESTEBAN (*maliciously*). Who gave me hints of how to write it? Who gave me chairs, and clothes, and men, but you, my little, darling wife?

MARIANA (*furious*). But even I could not give you wit, my love. Each day I watch your ears grow longer and more pointed. Some day they will fall down and slap your cheeks, like that... (*Gives him a resounding slap.*) ...and then you will remember Mariana.

ESTEBAN (*ruefully*). You are the whip I wear here at my belt, my sweet... (*Rubs his face.*) ...a whip that does not need my hand to wield its power.

MARIANA. Enough of arguments. The crowd will soon be here. Go out and hunt a prompter.

ESTEBAN (*scandalized*). At this hour? Have you no thought at all for my great art? Am I not the hero of this play? In a short time I must walk across that stage, and even now my poor heart is beating in my chest, and see my hands... (*Wiggles them loosely.*) ...shaking at the wrist.

MARIANA (*firmly*). Am I not the tragic lady of this play? I will not speak a line of your great drama until a man is safe within that box.

ESTEBAN (*imploring aid from Heaven*). Why did I marry such a woman, who loves an argument more than her soul's salvation?

MARIANA (*also imploring Heaven*). Why did I marry such a lazy fool who would rather sit in the sun and watch the goats feed on the mountain side than make an honest living for his family?
(LORENZO *opens the platform door and sticks his head through.*)

LORENZO. There are some people coming up the hill.

MARIANA (*giving a startled shriek. Runs toward bedroom door*). The audience! And I not dressed!

ESTEBAN (*stopping her*). Mariana, Lorenzo can find the man we need. (*As* MARIANA *pauses, he turns to* LORENZO.) My son, we need a prompter. Go into the town and search for one.

MARIANA. Bring back a man who can read, and not some ignorant fool.

LORENZO (*comes out on the platform, a large square piece of red velvet in his hands*). I have already spoken to Don Pancho's son, Ramón. The one who peddles silks and threads to all the women in the towns nearby. He can read, yes, and write, too.

MARIANA (*her eyes fixed on the velvet, and speaking in a strangled voice*). Lorenzo! Lorenzo, for what is that red velvet?

LORENZO (*innocently*). To cover the prompter's box, my mother, so that all the world shall know we give a play.

MARIANA (*stalking up to the platform*). Where did you get it? Where did you find that strip of goods? (ESTEBAN *frantically signals to* LORENZO *to keep quiet.*)

LORENZO (*looking curiously at his father*). What is it, sir? Why do you not speak out? I can not read such wavings of the hands.
(ESTEBAN *sinks down on one of the benches with a helpless gasp.*)

MARIANA (*swings on him*). So! It was you who gave it to him, eh? Well, search your brain for clever, useless answers. Where did you find the velvet?

ESTEBAN (*pleadingly*). Mariana, you have not worn that dress in many years. Not once have you worn it since our wedding day.

MARIANA (*slowly*). My dress. My beautiful red dress. The dress I wore when I first met the man I loved. (*Glares at him.*) From which part did you cut it?

LORENZO (*helpfully*). From the back. (*Turns around and makes an effort to show her how high up the cut came.*) You could replace the goods with a piece of red silk. Besides, when you are talking to your friends, they would not peer behind to see the difference.

MARIANA (*bursting into tears*). Oh, love of God and all the little angels! When was a woman so afflicted with such fools for a family?

ESTEBAN (*awkwardly patting her shoulder*). I know, my sweet, my heart's queen, my little cooing dove, that you have kept it out of sentiment. But you have other gowns that you first wore at our early meetings.

MARIANA (*jerking away from him*). I said I wore it when I met the man I loved, not the ass I married! (*Blazing out at them.*) Get out of my sight, the two of you! Oh, saints in Heaven, you and your plays and goats, and my red velvet gown. (*Her voice drops to a quiet deadly tone.*) I will make you pay for this, my friend.
(*Girls' voices are heard in the street.*)

LORENZO (*excitedly*). We must draw the curtains. The audience arrives.

MARIANA. Will you leave before I break a piece of wood across your heads? (*Screams.*) Get out!

ESTEBAN (*jumps up on platform*). We had best leave, my son. Your mother feels a little nervous.
(*As they start out* ESTEBAN *looks at* MARIANA *who has walked to the gate and has her back turned to them. He runs to the prompter's box, drapes it with the velvet, then hastily pulls the curtains as the girls appear at the gate. He and* LORENZO *disappear through the platform door.*)

MARIANA (*opening the gate*). Enter, enter. Our house is yours.
(ESTER, LOLA, *and* CARMEN *enter. Their skirts are of striped material, their blouses very white and clean. Their hair falls in two plaits over their shoulders, and*

they possess the wild, shy beauty of young deer. All three have on shawls. When they speak their voices are high and shrill and sweet, and they have the habit of giggling behind their hands.)

ESTER. Here is our money, Doña Mariana.

LOLA. Will Lorenzo play a part?
(*All giggle at* LOLA's *boldness.*)

MARIANA (*beaming on them*). He will indeed.

CARMEN. May we sit anywhere we like?

MARIANA (*nodding*). Wherever you may choose to sit save in the rocking-chairs. They are for Doña Berta and Don Pepe.
(*The girls giggle as they find their places.* RAMON *comes to the gate.*)
(RAMON *is very handsome and knows it. He wears a stiff straw hat, a bright pink shirt, a black tie, brown trousers, and shoes that are more orange than yellow with button tops. His voice drips with personality.*)

RAMON. Is this the house of one Esteban Elizondo? Is this the house where there will be a play?

MARIANA (*gazing thoughtfully at him. To her, any new man is subject to conquest. It is perfectly harmless. She has never been unfaithful to* ESTEBAN. *She just likes to know that she could be if she wanted to*). So you are old Don Pancho's youngest son, Ramón.

RAMON (*makes her a low bow*). Your servant, señorita.

MARIANA (*smiling faintly*). I am Lorenzo's mother.

RAMON (*steps back*). Impossible! Why, you do not look so old as he. (*Lifts her hand.*) Allow me to press a kiss upon your hand from my dirty mouth.
(ESTEBAN, *sticking his head through the curtain, sees this gallant gesture and glares at them.*)

LOLA (*tittering*). Good evening, Don Esteban.

ESTEBAN (*grumpily*). You may not speak to me. I am not here. I am behind the curtain. (*Trying to show his authority.*) Mariana! Take his money and let him in.

MARIANA (*shrugs her shoulders*). He is the prompter.

ESTEBAN (*snapping at her*). Then he should be safely in his box, and you changing your gown. I will not have you roll the eye at every man who comes along.

RAMON. Would you be jealous of me, Don Esteban, and I only a poor peddler of women's goods?

ESTEBAN. I trust no man when Mariana rolls the eye. Lorenzo will stand at the gate.
(LORENZO *sticks his head through the curtains below* ESTEBAN'S.)

CARMEN. Good evening, Lorenzo.
(*The three girls giggle.*)

LORENZO. Good evening, Carmen, Lola... (*He gives a deep sigh for he is in love with* ESTER.) ...Good evening, Ester.

ESTEBAN (*sharply*). You may not speak to them. Are they not the audience? Are you not on the stage? You must stand at the gate and take the money in your mother's place.

LORENZO. But I can not stand at the gate and learn my part.

ESTEBAN (*yelling, since the poor man is irritated beyond endurance*). You should know your part! You will stand where I direct you. (*Gives him a push, and* LORENZO, *who is holding the curtains, swings out, falling off the platform, taking curtains and* ESTEBAN *with him. The girls scream and stand up on their bench.* MARIANA *and* RAMON *laugh.*)

ESTEBAN (*from below the mass of curtains*). Help us up!

LORENZO (*wailing*). Ay, father, you are sitting on my stomach.

MARIANA (*strolling over to the jerking heap of curtains*). Do I stay and take the money, my dear love?

ESTEBAN. You will change your gown.

RAMON. Here comes Don Pepe climbing up the hill. He will enjoy this drama. Not every hero can be wrapped in blankets.

(*A low murmur of voices from the road at the left can be heard growing louder and louder.*)

MARIANA. Speak quickly, my sweet turnip.

ESTEBAN (*frantically fighting with the curtains*). Help me up and you can own the goat.

MARIANA (*trying to hide her laughter*). Will you lend your hand, Ramón?

RAMON (*makes her a deep bow*). For you, dear lady, I would cage the sun in a crystal lamp, and borrow a star's five points to bind your hair.

LORENZO (*moaning*). Father, will you get off my stomach?

ESTEBAN (*as* RAMON *helps him up*). I will, when peddling fools remember how to act instead of speaking airy verses to the moon's left ear. (*Moving threateningly toward* RAMON.) As for you, my fine friend...

MARIANA (*hastily*). No time for speeches now. Aid Lorenzo with the curtain.

LOLA. May we help?

MARIANA. You may indeed with Don Pepe at our gates. I will hold him off until the task is finished.

RAMON (*gallantly*). My arm, lady?

MARIANA (*takes it with a smile meant to infuriate* ESTEBAN). Thank you, Ramón.
(*They exit through the gate.* ESTEBAN *hangs over it gazing jealously after them.* LORENZO *is putting up the curtain.*)

ESTER (*watching* LORENZO). You are very strong.

LORENZO. In all the valley there is no man so strong as I.

LOLA (*helping* LORENZO *with the curtain*). So Ester said yesterday. (*She giggles.*)

ESTER (*snaps at her*). You have no right to repeat my words.

LORENZO (*forgetting the curtain steps down from the platform in front of* ESTER). You spoke of me...yesterday?

CARMEN (*helping* LOLA *with the curtain*). You are the constant subject of her speech.

ESTER. Who gave you leave to tell such tales of me? (*Flounces over and sits on bench.* LORENZO *follows her.*)

LORENZO (*softly*). Will you be at the plaza tonight?

ESTER (*turns her back on him*). I do not know.

LORENZO (*moving around to see her face, but she promptly turns her back again*). If you are there, will you walk around with me?

ESTER (*pleasantly shocked*). Alone?

LORENZO (*boldly*). Alone. Three times around.

ESTER (*gasping for breath*). But that would say to all the world that we two were engaged!

LORENZO (*sitting beside her*). My father soon will have enough to buy a goat, and then two goats, and then a herd. He will give me money to buy a wedding gown for you, and slippers... small white slippers. (*As the final tantalizing bit, since any beggar could have real flowers.*) And orange blossoms fashioned out of wax.

ESTER (*turning away her head*). Who can marry anyone without a house?

LORENZO. We will have a house with floors of soft blue tile. There will be a patio with white flowers growing in it. And, at night, when the moon is shining, there will be a light of pure green silver on your face. The locusts will hum their scratchy tunes, and the gray mocking-birds will wake and sing to us.

ESTER. What will they sing?

LORENZO. Of other lands they've seen beneath the moon. Of dusky jewels shining on white arms. Of fields of flowers sweet in bloom. Night-blooming jasmine, and the pale filigree of oleander. Of lilies, fragile as your hands, and blossoming thorn too sweet for any man to know its fragrance.

ESTER (*moves to another bench and stands looking down at it*). Is that all?

LORENZO (*following her*). Perhaps they will sing of mountains like purple ships against the soft pink evening sky... of cities that are pearls on the golden breasts of distant valleys...

ESTER (*whispering*). Is that all?

LORENZO (*softly*). Perhaps they will sing of blue tiled floors, and you and me. (*Catches up her hand.*) Will you walk around the plaza, three times, alone?

ESTER (*facing him and once again the flirt*). With you?

LORENZO. With me.

ESTER. Tonight?

LORENZO (*steps closer to her*). Tonight.

ESTER (*draws back. She hears voices in the street*). There is Don Pepe.

LORENZO (*catching her wrist*). But will you come?

ESTER (*jerks away from him, then laughs up into his face*). Perhaps! (*Runs up to* LOLA *and* CARMEN *at the platform.*)

LORENZO (*catches his breath, then flings back his head and begins to sing triumphantly*).

Shadow of our lord, St. Peter,
The river lures me,
The river lures me.
And thus your love
Would my poor love allure...
My love allure.

ESTEBAN (*turning*). Stop your crackling. Behind the curtains with you, and you, señoritas, to your chairs. (*The girls giggle as they return to their bench.*)

LORENZO (*as he passes* ESTER, *whispers*). Tonight? (ESTER *tosses her head at him.* LORENZO *and* ESTEBAN *disappear behind the curtains as* DON PEPE, *the mayor of The Three Marys enters with* DOÑA BERTA *on his arm. She is a large impressive looking woman, while he is a tiny spry little man. A crowd of men and women follow them. The men wear various colored bandannas knotted about their throats, and the white pyjama suits of the tropics, while the women are in colors as brilliant as the birds of the jungle country. They are all in a very gay humor, ready to enjoy the play.*)

DON PEPE (*impressively*). I have not seen a play upon the stage since I was last in the United States. (*He leads* DOÑA BERTA *to the rockers.*) Good evening, Carmen, Lola, Ester.

LOLA. Do they have plays upon a stage in the United States?

DON PEPE. They have the photographs of people who walk across a screen and talk like you or me.

CARMEN (*giggles*). Oh, Don Pepe, what a tease you are.

DON PEPE. And what is more they can make their water hot or cold with merely the turning of a handle.

MAN FROM CROWD. Now, Don Pepe, would you play with us?

DON PEPE (*with a luxurious sigh*). Ay, it is an education to travel.

DOÑA BERTA. I prefer my own bed every night.

ESTER. Is it true that girls can walk with men, even though they are not engaged?

DON PEPE. It is indeed.

DOÑA BERTA (*scandalized*). A most immoral custom. Put not such foreign thoughts in our girls' heads, Don Pepe.

DON PEPE (*rises and makes her a low bow, then sits down again*). Always your obedient servant, Doña Berta.

MARIANA (*to* RAMON). You had best into the prompter's box, while I change my gown.

RAMON. If you need aid...

MARIANA (*tosses her head*). Then I will not call for you, my saucy lad. (*She goes into the bedroom right.*)

RAMON (*as he steps into the box the audience claps loudly. He holds up a modest hand*). I am but the prompter, my friends.

MAN FROM CROWD. Long life to the prompter. (*The audience claps loudly again.* RAMON *makes another bow, and lowers himself into the prompter's box.*)

LOLA (*whispers*). Ester, did Lorenzo ask you anything?

ESTER. Why should I tell you what was said?

CARMEN. We would keep your words as secret as a priest at confessional.

DOÑA BERTA. What would you keep secret, Miss?

CARMEN. Ester spoke with Lorenzo all alone.

DOÑA BERTA (*scandalized*). What?

DON PEPE (*startled*). Eh?

ESTER (*defensively*). Lola, Carmen, and Don Esteban were here.

LOLA. But just we three. That is almost the same as being alone.

DOÑA BERTA. That is your wild advice taking root, Don Pepe.

DON PEPE. Girls and boys must speak together. How else would marriages arrange themselves?

DOÑA BERTA. When I was young, girls listened to their parents.

MAN FROM CROWD. Is that why you have remained a spinster, Doña Berta?
(*Loud laughter from the crowd.*)

DRUNK IN CROWD (*sings tune of* LA CUCARACHA).*

All the maidens are of gold
And the married ones of silver.
All the widows are of copper
And the others merely tin.
La cucaracha, la cucaracha...

DOÑA BERTA (*stands. She is furious*). Is this the gathering place of drunks?

DON PEPE (*standing*). Take out the fool.

DRUNK. I paid my money...

DON PEPE (*in his most thundering voice*). What did you say?

DRUNK. I said... I need another drink. (*He staggers to the gate, then staggers back and shakes his finger at* DOÑA BERTA, *as he sings tauntingly.*) And the others are of lead...
(DON PEPE *signals to a man in the crowd who drags the drunk outside the gate and then returns to his own bench.*)

DOÑA BERTA (*reseating herself*). Such common men deserve to stay in jail, Don Pepe.

DON PEPE (*flinging out his hands*). He stays in jail so much, Doña Berta, that he keeps his clothes there and calls it his hotel. I gave him the key to his cell yesterday. I became quite bored with locking it to keep him in, and then unlocking it to let him out.

* See above, p. 64.

(LORENZO *sticks his head through the curtains. There is loud applause from the audience.*)

LORENZO (*grinning and nodding his head, then to the prompter*). Ramón. (RAMON *sticks his head above the prompter's box.*) Can you perform on the harmonica?

RAMON. Alas, my only talent is for the drums.

LORENZO (*woefully*). But who will play the applause music?

MAN FROM CROWD. We will sing it for you.

LORENZO. Thank you, my friend. (*Steps in front of the curtain.*)

AUDIENCE (*sings lustily to tune of* LA CUCARACHA).

Now the duck is in the pot
Bubbling for the fire is hot,
Lifts his head and calls for savor,
Adds an onion for the flavor. (*They applaud loudly.*)

LORENZO (*bows and shakes his own hands over his head to the audience*). This is a tragedy of laughter, and a comedy of tears.

MAN IN CROWD. Long live the drama!
(*Shouting and applause from the crowd.*)

LORENZO. Its story I need not tell you, for you will see it for yourselves upon the stage. We ask you to laugh where laughter is needed, and for your tears where you

should weep. If you go home contented, our labor has been repaid. (*Retires behind the curtain.*)
(*More shouts and applause from the audience.*)

MARIANA (*strolls in from the bedroom, dressed in a brilliant costume and with flowers in her hair*). I am the heroine. Will some kind gentleman aid me to the platform?

DON PEPE (*hastening to her*). May I be of service? (*Whispering as he lifts her to the platform.*) Was there enough to buy the goat?

MARIANA (*laughs*). Quite enough, my friend. Thank you. (*Disappears behind the curtain.*)

LOLA (*nervously tittering*). Oh, I am so excited.

CARMEN. Someone is pulling back the curtain.
(ESTEBAN, *a large straw hat on his head, a gaily striped blanket over one shoulder, and carrying a gun, now pulls back the curtains. There is loud applause from the audience.*)

CROWD (*sings*).

Beans and corn and sweet potatoes,
Add a touch of red tomatoes.
Forget your sobs and your great sorrow,
We will all be drunk tomorrow.

(ESTEBAN *strikes an heroic attitude. There is a silence. Again he strikes an attitude. Again there is silence. He leans over and knocks on the prompter's box.*)

RAMON (*pops out his head*). Eh?

ESTEBAN (*impatiently*). Well...begin.

RAMON (*blankly*). Were you ready?

ESTEBAN (*takes a deep breath*). St. Peter give me patience! (*Thunders.*) We are ready!

RAMON (*lightly*). I have no book.

ESTEBAN. And you call yourself a prompter!

RAMON. No, a peddler. (*Seizing the opportunity, he stands and faces the audience.*) Ladies of the audience, I have silks and satins, wedding gowns and gowns for mourning, threads and pins to make you beautiful...

ESTEBAN (*screams*). Enough! (*More quietly.*) This is a noble drama, not a sale of women's clothes. (*Calling through the door.*) Lorenzo, the book.

LORENZO (*tosses the book through the curtains*). Here you are, father.

ESTEBAN (*hands it to* RAMON *who sinks down into the box. Again* ESTEBAN *strikes an attitude*). Begin! (*The prompter speaks rapidly in a clear, monotonous voice with the actors, but he is usually just a word ahead of them.*)

EST. AND RAMON. I am a soldier home from war...

AUDIENCE. Bravo!

EST. AND RAMON. I am the bravest man in Mexico!

AUDIENCE. Long live the Republic! Long live Mexico!

EST. AND RAMON. I am returned after twenty years to see my wife and child.

MAN IN CROWD. The Revolution only lasted eight years.

ESTEBAN (*glaring at him*). Is this my war or yours? (*Here* ESTEBAN *reads one speech and* RAMON *another.*)

RAMON. How I love my beautiful wife...

ESTEBAN. I am returned after thirty years... (*Bangs on prompter's box.*) You are ahead of me, Ramon.

RAMON. Did I know you were going to repeat? (*Reading.*) To see my wife and son.

ESTEBAN (*exasperated*). I have already said that.

RAMON. Well, say it again.

LORENZO (*sticking head through the door*). Father! (*Crooks a finger at him.*)

ESTEBAN (*walks to the door*). Well, what do you want?

LORENZO (*in a loud whisper*). You entered too soon. We are supposed to be ahead of you.

ESTEBAN (*who is rapidly losing his patience*). I wrote this play, and if I wish to be ahead of you, I will be first.

LORENZO. Mother says that if she does not enter now she will not act at all.

ESTEBAN (*who recognizes defeat when he sees it. He sighs*). Very well. (*Comes down to the edge of the platform and speaks to the audience.*) Pretend I have not been here. I will return in a little while. (*Goes through door to much applause from the audience.*) (MARIANA *and* LORENZO *enter.*)

MAR. AND RAMON. I fear your father soon returns from the distant wars.

LOR. AND RAMON. Father? You told me that he died long years before I was born.

MAR. AND RAMON. There is a weight within my breast. I have always felt it there before I saw your father. (*Loud stamping noise behind platform door.*) I hear him now, the ghostly beat of horse's hoofs. (*Falls to her knees.*) Oh, Holy Virgin, save me from his wrath.

LOR. AND RAMON. I will see who comes. (*He runs out through door.*)

MAR. AND RAMON (*she beats her chest*). Ay, ay, ay.

LOR. AND RAMON (LORENZO *enters immediately wearing a false mustache*). My wife!

MAR. AND RAMON. My husband! (*They fall into each other's arms. She draws back.*) I may no longer call you husband.

LOR. AND RAMON. What news is this? What sad words beat against my brain?

MAR. AND RAMON. I fear Lorenzo's father does return today.

LOR. AND RAMON. You told me he was dead.

MAR. AND RAMON. And so I thought, but in the cards I read of a dark man, a dangerous man, and he is very dark, and very dangerous.

LOR. AND RAMON. Your speech has stabbed me...

LORENZO (*in a loud whisper to* RAMON). Speak louder, Ramón.

LOR. AND RAMON (RAMON *is laughing so hard his words are muffled*). My heart is rent in twain.

LORENZO (*to* RAMON). How can I hear you if you laugh, you fool?

LOR. AND RAMON (*both begin to shout, but* RAMON *wins*). I die, I die...I am dead! (LORENZO *stretches himself carefully out on the platform.*)

MAR. AND RAMON. Help, help, he is dead. (*She kneels beside him, lifts up her arms, then looks at the audience.*)

MARIANA. Silence, please. This is the sad speech.

MAR. AND RAMON. Oh, saints in Heaven, protect me from the wrath of man. Guard in your arms this poor sweet soul whose only sin... (*She gives a long sob.*) ... was loving me too much.

ESTER (*wailing*). Oh, Carmen, Lorenzo is dead!

LORENZO (*sitting up*). I will return to life if you will walk around the plaza with me.

MARIANA (*pushes him down*). Lie down, you fool. You are dead. (*To* RAMON.) What happens next?

RAMON. You carry him out.

MARIANA (*in a loud whisper*). Lorenzo, this is where you go out. (LORENZO *stands.*) Walk like a ghost. Remember, you are dead.
(LORENZO, *in as ghost-like a manner as possible, vanishes through the platform door.*)

MAR. AND RAMON. I am a widow once again. Oh, Heaven, Oh, Saints, Oh, Love. (*She follows* LORENZO *out.* ESTEBAN *enters with his face turned to the side, proving that he can not see* MARIANA.)

ESTEBAN (*to the audience*). You remember that I am home, so we will continue from where I was... (*he glares at the platform door*) ... interrupted. I am ready to begin, Ramón.

EST. AND RAMON. I bear upon my chest the scars of war. (*Loud applause from the audience.*) Once I was wounded.... (*Loud applause.* ESTEBAN *holds up his hand.*)

ESTEBAN. You are not supposed to clap there.

EST. AND RAMON. Once I was wounded, but my enemy was cut to bits, and now I am home again to feast my eyes upon the beauty of my wife. (*Knocks on the door.*) Are all within here deaf?

LORENZO (*without the mustache, enters*). Father! (*Falls to his knees.*)

EST. AND RAMON (*draws back with dramatic surprise*). And who are you?

LOR. AND RAMON. Your son.

EST. AND RAMON. My son? Your age?

LOR. AND RAMON. Nineteen.

ESTER. Lorenzo! you told me you were twenty-two.

DON PEPE. This is a play, child, not a truth.

EST. AND RAMON (*with a glare for the interruption*). A son of mine nineteen, and I from home for thirty years?

MAN IN CROWD. You said twenty the first time.

ESTEBAN. Did I not write this play? If I choose to change the date then I change the date, with no advice from you!

EST. AND RAMON. Where hides the woman you call mother, and whom I once called wife!

ESTEBAN (*to the audience*). You can applaud for that. (*Loud applause.* ESTEBAN *modestly waving his hand.*) Thank you, my friends.

EST. AND RAMON. Where is she?
(MARIANA *enters.*)

MAR. AND RAMON. Ay, Federico!

EST. AND RAMON. Ysabela, my love...

MAR. AND RAMON. My husband! (*They embrace.*)

EST. AND RAMON (*he draws back from her*). One moment! Explain how it is that I have a son nineteen, and I from home... (*he comes down and glares at the man in the crowd*) ... forty years!

MAR. AND RAMON. I thought that you were dead, completely dead.

EST. AND RAMON. Kneel down.

MAR. AND RAMON (*she kneels*). I was young and beautiful, and weak to a man's whisper.

EST. AND RAMON. I must commune within my mind, secret and alone.

ESTEBAN (*goes down and faces audience*). What shall I do? What would you do, my friends?

MAN IN CROWD. Shoot her!

ANOTHER MAN. Chop off her head!

DOÑA BERTA (*in a trembling voice*). Forgive her.

ESTEBAN (*raps on prompter's box*). What do I do now?

RAMON. You choke her.

EST. AND RAMON (*he returns and begins to choke* MARIANA). So shall all men deal with unfaithful wives. (*Loud applause from the audience.* ESTEBAN *bows and goes down to edge of platform, shaking his own hands above his head.*)

AUDIENCE (*singing*).

Hungry now the neighbor's look,
Stand and wait and watch it cook.
But, alas, they must not eat it.
Bravo! Bravo!!!

ESTEBAN. Thank you, my friends. (*Goes back and finishes choking* MARIANA. *She falls dead.*)

EST. AND RAMON. So am I revenged. (*He kicks her.*)

MARIANA (*sits up angrily*). That kick was not in the play!

ESTEBAN. Shh . . . lie down. You are dead.

MARIANA. Not too dead to deal with you, you ancient eater of cow's meat. (*Reaches out and grasps one of the vases on the prompter's box and throws it at him.*

Scene from THE RED VELVET GOAT

MARIANA: My husband! I may no longer call you husband.

He ducks, and it smashes on the floor. She screams.) Ay, it was my own vase! I thought it was Doña Berta's.

DOÑA BERTA (*stands*). So I am not only insulted, but my property is destroyed as well. I stay no longer here! (*Sweeps out of the patio with hurt dignity.*)
(*The audience rises.*)

ESTEBAN (*wringing his hands*). But the play is not finished. I have still a beautiful speech.

MARIANA (*jumps down from the platform*). Say it alone! I am finished with your drama. (*Runs into bedroom right.*)

RAMON (*climbs out of the prompter's box*). As for me, I prefer a good bottle of beer in the saloon. I have money, my friends. Who joins me?
(*With much cheering the audience, with the exception of* DON PEPE, LOLA, CARMEN, *and* ESTER, *press forward to shake* ESTEBAN'S *hand, and then follow* RAMON *through the gate.*)

ESTEBAN (*sits down on the edge of the platform*). My beautiful play.

DON PEPE (*comfortingly*). It was an excellent drama, my friend. I think that we can arrange about the goat. (*To the girls.*) Shall I walk home with these three pretty flowers?

LOLA (*giggles*). Ay, Don Pepe.

CARMEN. Will you tell us all about the United States?

DON PEPE (*beaming*). With the greatest of pleasure.

LORENZO (*who has worked his way around to* ESTER). Ester.

ESTER (*earnestly*). When you died I knew the truth.

LORENZO. Will you be on the plaza tonight?

ESTER (*stamps her foot*). No.

LORENZO (*crestfallen*). You . . . won't?

ESTER. Not unless you should be there, too. (*Runs out through the gate.*)

LORENZO. Ester! (*Runs out after her.*)

DON PEPE. My three flowers have shrunk to two . . . one for each arm.

(*He extends his crooked arms and the girls take them.*)

LOLA (*as they exit through the gate*). Do they have such beautiful dramas in the United States?

(ESTEBAN *sinks his chin in his hands and takes a long sniffling breath.* MARIANA *enters, dressed in a bridal gown. She parades up and down in front of him.*)

ESTEBAN (*sighs*). The play is finished, but at least we have enough to buy the goat. (*Notices her for the first time.*) What are you wearing?

MARIANA. A bridal gown, which you could see if you were not so blind, my fool.

ESTEBAN. Have I seen that gown before?

MARIANA. I think not. It has only just been purchased. (*Preens herself.*)

ESTEBAN (*springing up*). From Ramón? (*He catches her wrist.*)

MARIANA (*pulling her hand away*). From the peddler of silks and satins, threads and pins, to make all ladies beautiful.

ESTEBAN (*narrowing his eyes*). With what did you pay for that gown?

MARIANA (*touching her dress lightly*). With the money that I took in at the door.

ESTEBAN (*squeaking*). The money for my goat?

MARIANA. No, my love. (*Jerks the velvet from the prompter's box and holds it out toward him.*) The money to replace an ancient gown of bright red velvet. ESTEBAN *grasps his head and moans as*

THE CURTAINS CLOSE

AZTECA

A TRAGEDY OF PRE-CONQUEST MEXICO

THE CHARACTERS

As originally produced by The Carolina Playmakers at Chapel Hill, North Carolina, on April 25, 1936.

XOCHITL, *a novitiate* . . . . Ellen Deppe
FIRST PRIESTESS . . . . Mary Haynsworth
SECOND PRIESTESS . . . . Patty Penn
THIRD PRIESTESS . . . . Ruth Mengel
HUALPA, *a warrior* . . . . John Hardie
TULA, *the High-Priestess* . . . Josephine Oettinger
MAXTLA, *an Aztecan noble, father of Xochitl and Tecuichpe* . . . . Al Nooger
TECUICHPE, *Xochitl's younger sister* . Mildred Howard

THE SCENE: A garden of the great temple dedicated to The Earth Mother, on the outskirts of Tenochtitlan, now Mexico City.

THE TIME: Late afternoon in autumn of the year 1412 (Christian calendar).

THE SCENE

The garden of the great temple of the Goddess who was called in Aztecan the Earth Mother. *The temple itself forms the left wall of the garden, and a large, square door leads to it. It is sunset, and there is a dignified grandeur in the simplicity of the altar which is made beautiful only through lines and angles, not through curves.*

This altar, vaguely suggestive of a low table, is placed on top of a platform to which lead three steps. Back of the platform, and slightly higher, is a great well... a great bottomless well... into which are thrown the bodies of those who have been sacrificed to the Goddess.

It is the year of the Christian calendar 1412, and the opening of the curtain reveals four young priestesses kneeling in the garden making flower wreaths for their hair. The four girls are pretty little things whose lives have been dedicated by their parents to the temple which they serve. If it were a Christian country they would be called nuns. They are dressed in pink, blue, yellow, and white. The one dressed in white is a novitiate. Her name is Xochitl, *which means "a flower," and she has the serene beauty of a white rose. Seeing her one thinks of a mountain in the far distance, placid and distinct against the sky, yet capable of a dark and terrible aspect with the setting sun.*

First Priestess. Lend me a flower for my wreath, Xochitl.

Second Priestess (*teasingly*). Xochitl is a flower, and a flower is Xochitl.

Xochitl. Do not tease if I wear a flower for a name. There have been queens named Xochitl, and once an Empress.

Third Priestess (*knowingly*). But legend has dipped her name in blood. Men, they say, killed themselves, having glimpsed her beauty.

Second Priestess (*gayly*). But no man shall kill himself for this small Xochitl.

(Xochitl *glances quickly at her and then away, with a sly knowing smile.*)

Xochitl (*with assumed indifference*). Has any nun within these cloistered walls ever been loved by mortal man?

Third Priestess. They say that once a priestess loved a man...

First Priestess (*looking over her shoulder toward the temple*). Hush! Those are forbidden words.

Xochitl. Some day I shall hear the legend. Why not now?

Second Priestess. Are we not dedicated to the Earth, our mighty mother? For us no more of love, no, nor any other thing that walks abroad through the great world outside.

XOCHITL (*pleading*). Tell me the tale. Was she fair?

THIRD PRIESTESS. They say he met her in this garden, and here they were found in each other's arms.

XOCHITL. And then?

SECOND PRIESTESS. They were thrown alive into the well.

XOCHITL (*with awe*). They must have known a great and glorious love if they could die for it.

FIRST PRIESTESS. Legend says at night the wood doves call the names of those two unfortunates. (*Holds up her wreath.*) But, see, my wreath is finished. This will be your first great sacrifice, young Xochitl. Does your heart flutter at the thought of what you are about to see?

XOCHITL (*trying to collect her thoughts and focus her attention on what is being said*). Who is the chosen one to have her soul sent into the arms of the Earth Mother?

THIRD PRIESTESS. That no one knows until the hour itself. Then Tula, the high-priestess, in the frenzy of the hour hears the soundless voice of the Earth Mother ringing in her ears, and so the choice is made.

XOCHITL (*fearfully*). Will it be ... one of us?

SECOND PRIESTESS. Never yet has one of us been chosen. Always it has been some maiden of the town ...

THIRD PRIESTESS. And once a man.

XOCHITL (*amazed*). A man?

SECOND PRIESTESS. A man. A warrior, and brave, and very handsome.

THIRD PRIESTESS (*with the artful innocence of the born gossip*). I think that Tula chose him because she feared that she would grow to love him.

FIRST PRIESTESS (*sharply*). Enough of this, and this is blasphemy indeed! Enough, I say! (*More gently to* XOCHITL.) And now, child, we will do the service once again, so that you shall not falter in your part. Take you the words of Tula, for knowing that, you will know all.

(XOCHITL *rises and stands in the center, the others grouped about her.*)

PRIESTESS (*chanting*). All glory to the earth.

XOCHITL (*there grows behind her words a hidden tragic force which the others lack. It seems very difficult for her to speak the words*). All glory to the Mighty Mother.

PRIESTESSES. Thus speak we, the dedicate.

XOCHITL. Keep within us the purity of wind and rain.

PRIESTESSES. Keep from us the lightning and the thunder.

XOCHITL. Keep from us the temptation of any mortal love.

PRIESTESSES. Let us remain the flowers of this garden.

XOCHITL (*finding it more and more difficult to continue*). Let us together as a single voice adore you, Earth and Mother.

PRIESTESSES. Here forever let us stay, warm against your heart.

XOCHITL (*her voice very low*). So speak we, the dedicate. (*She suddenly presses her hands against her forehead, her wreath of flowers falling unheeded to the ground. The* PRIESTESSES *stare up at her with curious concern as she speaks, the words forced out of her mouth.*) No, no, this is enough. I know the service. Let me rest until the hour of sacrifice.

FIRST PRIESTESS (*rising*). You are ill, oh, Xochitl?

XOCHITL (*snatching at the excuse*). Yes... yes I am ill.

SECOND PRIESTESS (*all are standing*). Let us bring Tula...

THIRD PRIESTESS. Let us bring Tula, the mother-priestess...

FIRST PRIESTESS. With her herbs she shall cure you.

PRIESTESSES. Let us bring Tula to you.

XOCHITL (*smiles wanly at them. They have surrounded her, and her outstretched arms are resting on theirs*). Not for me the subtle herbs of Tula. No medicine has she for a heart that is heavy with grief.

SECOND AND THIRD PRIESTESSES. Tell us, oh, Xochitl...

THIRD PRIESTESS. We are your friends.

XOCHITL (*leaves them and goes up on platform*). My heart was a singing bird, but now the song is forgotten, and the bird is snared in a net.

PRIESTESSES. Xochitl, the lonely and sad.

XOCHITL. In other years, before I knew the shadow of these walls, there was no maiden in Tolan so happy as this Xochitl. I knew the ecstasy of the blue sky, the poignant beauty of a cloud, for I was young, and love was a stranger still.

PRIESTESSES. Happy Xochitl, in those days so long ago.

XOCHITL. Then Love came knocking at my father's door. Love was strange and beautiful. Love was fresh as the green months of spring.

PRIESTESSES. All the world was fair, and Xochitl found new rapture in every budding day.

XOCHITL. With each passing hour love grew stronger still, and I had shy sweet thoughts of future joy. But then...

PRIESTESSES. But then...?

XOCHITL. My father told me the dread secret hidden in his heart so many years. That on my eighteenth birthday, by my dead mother's vow, I was to enter here as a novitiate.

PRIESTESSES. Now ended hope and future's golden fancy.

XOCHITL AND PRIESTESSES. So farewell world, and farewell love, for love is a stranger here.
(XOCHITL *is looking toward the right, and now she represses a start, then looks down at the* PRIESTESSES *and smiles brightly at them.*)

XOCHITL. You say you are my friends? Then leave me here alone to dream in this old garden. Perhaps the doves will call the names of those two brave lovers... please.

FIRST PRIESTESS (*doubtfully*). Strange thoughts for a young girl, and dedicate to Mother Earth.

THIRD PRIESTESS. Let us leave her, sister. I, too, had dreams when I first came here.

SECOND PRIESTESS. We who can no longer dream should not begrudge her what she, too, will lose in time.

FIRST PRIESTESS. So be it. But if Tula finds you here, say that we left you, not that you sent us from you, for Tula has a dark and mighty anger that falls like thunder on the unprepared.

XOCHITL (*nervously*). I will heed your warning.

PRIESTESSES (*turn and go into the temple, chanting*). All glory to the sun and rain, those lovers of our Mother Earth. All glory to the flowers and trees, those children of our Mother Earth. And glorious, most glorious, the soul that at twilight shall see Her.

(XOCHITL, *her hand pressed against her heart, listens until their voices fade in the distance, then she walks right and lifts her arm in a signal for* HUALPA *to enter. He is a goodlooking boy in his early twenties, dressed in the uniform of his caste, that of a warrior. She is very obviously in love with him, and he is just as obviously not in love with her. When he enters she goes up to him, and putting her arms about him, leans against him.*)

XOCHITL. Hualpa. Hualpa, my beloved. (*Then she draws back and looks about her, frightened. When she turns back to him, she speaks softly and cautiously.*) You should not be here. Even now they are preparing for the sacrifice. If they found us two together, our death would be most horrible. I know. They were telling me of two who were found.

HUALPA. I am a warrior and used to danger. I had to speak to you.

XOCHITL (*looking at him with admiration*). I wish that I had courage, but lately Fear has followed me, until its shadow has enveloped me like a robe of night. For I have sinned against my vows in loving you, and you have sinned against the gods in loving me.

HUALPA. Luckily for us both, even sin must have an end.

XOCHITL (*not understanding his meaning*). There is no end save in the land of death for us, unless... (*She draws back frightened.*) But no! We would not dare!

HUALPA (*irritated*). You speak in riddles.

XOCHITL. No riddle this, if you mean to steal me from these walls. (*Flings out her arms.*) Back to the world once more. How beautiful, how glorious is the freedom of the world.

HUALPA. No freedom if I stole you. We would stand accursed in all men's eyes. (*He points to the temple.*) She would track us down. No matter where we went, the dark magic of the high-priestess, Tula, would blaze our footsteps in a very arc of light for her to read.

XOCHITL (*puzzled*). These are new fears trembling in you. Is there no strength left in all the love that you have sworn to me?

HUALPA (*harshly*). How can there be strength when love is dead?

XOCHITL (*after a slight pause, whispers*). Dead?

HUALPA. Yes, dead. And so I say that even sin must end, if we have sinned. (*He turns away from her.*) I loved you when you walked the world's wide path, but now you linger here within these walls, and I must follow other roads. What was between us two is ended. Love lightly taken is easily forgotten. You will forget, as I already have.

XOCHITL (*horrified*). Love lightly taken. So that is what the breaking of my vows has meant to you. Love lightly taken. How easily those words roll from your tongue. Love lightly taken... no, not taken, drawn, like water from a well, from this cup beating in my breast. (*Smiles bitterly.*) They say old cups shatter when too long in use. I can feel this one breaking now.

HUALPA. Hearts are not so fragile. At first there is a little pain, but hearts mend easily.

XOCHITL. At least in men they do.

HUALPA. I am a warrior. I am used to wounds. But you are a woman, soft as the petals of a flower. Soft things bruise, but even bruises heal.

XOCHITL (*dazed*). This is some horrible dream, sent as a punishment by Her who is the Earth. Soon I shall wake again and know that Hualpa loves me still. (*Desperately.*) Tell me that this is but a dream!

HUALPA. No dream but truth. We are done with dreaming, you and I. Here within these walls you must stand alone, forgetting Life. For you the Future is a long white road without a single turning. I... I am a man, and before me spread the corners of the world. For a little while my path and yours were one, but now the cross-roads beckon me away. So I have come to say good-by.

XOCHITL. Do not try to hide the truth from me. These walls shut out the world, but I remember how it was before I came to live in this bound garden. You have found other eyes that kindle with a flame at your approach, and other lips more honey-sweet than mine.

HUALPA (*taking her hand and speaking gently*). Why should I lie to you? We have been honest with each other since our first meeting. I had hoped to spare you added pain, but since you have found my secret out...

(*He turns away from her, as though trying to justify himself.*) I would have sons to follow me...to add more glory to my name.

XOCHITL (*quietly*). Who is she?

HUALPA. Your sister, the small Tecuichpe.

XOCHITL (*after a brief pause draws away from him*). Tecuichpe! Of all women, why did you choose her?

HUALPA. You make me cruel, when I would be kind.

XOCHITL. Tell me...tell me why my own sister?

HUALPA. Even before we learned that you were dedicated to this virgin temple, even then my heart told me the truth, that I loved not you but your small sister. On that day when they brought you here, I tried to weep, but Xochitl, can a man govern the beating of his heart, be master of the very breath he draws? I loved her then, and I love her now, far more than you have ever dared to love.

XOCHITL (*angrily*). How can you speak her name and think of love in the same moment's time? You said you loved me once...you swore it on our two clasped hands. Now that oath's forgotten like the winds of yesterday. And now you love Tecuichpe. (*Her voice breaks, and she adds pitifully.*) Poor small bloom of cotton, as soft and fragile as her name. How is it I can hate yet love her still?

Hualpa. I never loved you, Xochitl. I thought I did. All those vows I swore to you I meant when I was swearing them, but now I know what true love is. I know that it is all of beauty, and all the pain that beauty brings.

Xochitl. Pain? Shall I ever know again what pain is? I feel so strange, as though this body were a poor empty shell. My arms... (*Holds them out.*) ...see, they are steady. No trembling here, for dead things do not tremble, and I am dead. (*Without venom, but as a simple statement.*) You have killed me, Hualpa.

Hualpa (*bowing his head*). Perhaps in future years you will forgive, and know this is the better way. How far more terrible had our love stayed the same, yet with the shadow of these tall, gray walls between us.

Xochitl (*flinging her arms about him*). No, no! Take me away from here and love me still. In time you will forget her. It was my swift departure that left you helpless and alone, so that you had to turn to her for comforting. It is me you love, not her. My heart will not let me believe this awful thing. I know you loved me once. (*Sinks to her knees, her arms still about him. His face is turned away in pity.*) You will again. My arms are gentle as hers, my mouth as sweet. She can never love you as I do. Hualpa, Hualpa, say you love me still! (*Neither one sees* Tula *enter from the temple. Wearing the green of the royal house, she possesses both strength and dignity. Here is a rugged individualism, that, not knowing weakness in itself, cannot condone it in anyone else.*)

HUALPA (*puts his hand on* XOCHITL'S *head*). Poor Xochitl. Poor broken flower.

TULA (*coming forward, horrified*). What blasphemy is this!

XOCHITL (*drawing closer to* HUALPA *for protection*). Tula!

HUALPA (*dropping to his knees*). The high-priestess!

XOCHITL (*flings out her hand in supplication*). He only came to say good-by. Is that a sin? He came to say good-by.

TULA (*sternly*). Did I ask you why he came, or how?

HUALPA. Lady, she speaks true words...

TULA. Now this garden once again the breaking of a priestess' vows has witnessed. The wood doves must learn two new names at sunset....

XOCHITL (*pleading*). Have you no pity for a maiden's breaking heart?

HUALPA. The grimness of farewell has brought me here, and nothing more. I swear it.

TULA. The temple gates part man and maid forever.

XOCHITL. If you have ever loved, have pity on us.

TULA. Once love and I were dear familiar friends. But duty pressed cold hands upon my breast, and bound me with the chains of my stern vows. (*To* XOCHITL.) You say you love this man, but I loved *him* as the eagle loves its flying eagle-mate. We were two separate bodies with a single star for soul, yet duty was the grim, green spear between us, for I was dedicate to earth, and earth may gaze upon, but never touch the sky.

XOCHITL. He loved you, and you could let him go, loving him?

TULA. In the frenzy of the sacrifice I chose him whom I loved, and stretched him on that altar. My knife, my dark obsidian knife, drank deep of his bright red and wine-sweet blood. (*She pauses in the memory of that moment.*) You are young, Xochitl, very young to die. Because I once felt your pain, I give you the choice that I once had to make. (*Her voice becomes clear and cold.*) Your warrior's life upon the altar there at sunset, or your two lives together, now.

XOCHITL (*on a sobbing note*). No, no! Do not make me choose.

TULA (*turns to* HUALPA). Then you shall make the choice. If you love her, it will not be difficult. The two of you together, or you alone at sunset.
(HUALPA *looks from one woman to the other, and when he sees the expression, almost of triumph, on* XOCHITL's *face, he draws back.*)

XOCHITL (*half whispering*). Choose, Hualpa, for which ever way you choose, you will have died for me... for me, Hualpa... for me.

HUALPA (*after a moment of indecision turns and catches* TULA's *wrist*). There is another choice, lady.

(Snatching his knife from where it rests against his back he plunges it into her heart. She gasps and sinks forward, and he catches her as she falls.)

XOCHITL (*horrified*). What have you done! In just a little while the sacrifice . . . she will be missed . . . and we . . . oh, you have doomed us both, most horribly!

HUALPA (*swiftly stripping off* TULA's *great robe, and snatching up the mask, hands them to* XOCHITL). Put these on . . .

XOCHITL (*drawing back*). I? But those are sacred to the office of the high-priestess. For me to wear them would be blasphemy.

HUALPA (*coldly*). Better that you be missed than she.

XOCHITL (*frightened*). I do not understand.

HUALPA. Do as I tell you. For the sacrifice you must take her place. You know the ritual? (*She nods dumbly.*) Make no mistake. This is a dangerous road we walk, for if you fail, then we two are doomed. One must not fail the other.

XOCHITL (*emphatically*). And if I do not fail, what then? What of the afterwards? You will be gone and safe, but I? But what of me, left here within these walls?

HUALPA. There is no other way.

XOCHITL (*insinuatingly*). You could steal me out of here tonight.

HUALPA. No... no, you must not ask me that.

XOCHITL. Then let them find us. Let them do what they like to both of us. Better for me to die, knowing you dead, than for me to live, knowing you lost to me forever. That is my price. Freedom for both of us, or death most horrible.

HUALPA. How can you ask this, knowing that all my life long it will be your sister's love I crave, not yours?

XOCHITL. You will forget her. Did you not say yourself that you are a warrior and used to wounds, and that hearts mend most easily?

HUALPA. You leave me no choice at all.

XOCHITL. Then swear to me by ... (*she points to* TULA) ... by her terrible blood that you will turn to me and to no other all your life long.

HUALPA (*desperately*). I cannot swear.

XOCHITL (*with cold finality*). You must. With me is life itself. Together we have sinned.

HUALPA. Together we are damned.

XOCHITL. Together we are meshed in this dark web of crime....

HUALPA. Could not immediate death be a far sweeter thing?

XOCHITL. You hold Death in your arms. No pulse beats now in that white throat, no breath disturbs those delicate red lips. Look on her. Look on Death and make your choice.

HUALPA (*looks down at* TULA, *then covers his face with his hands. There is a moment's pause, then beaten, he draws a deep breath and stands, lifting* TULA *in his arms*). What shall I do with her?

XOCHITL. Her lover's body was thrown into the well. Let us throw her after him. Perhaps in that shadowed land behind the sun her spirit will find his. (*With* TULA *in his arms,* HUALPA *climbs to the well's edge and peers down into its depths.*) Hurry. There is little time left to us. (*He throws* TULA's *body over the brink, then stands there, his head bowed, his hands clenched at his side. In a moment he comes down the steps, while* XOCHITL *puts on the robe, the mask still dangling in her hand.*) You will come for me tonight when the moon is above the outer gate.

HUALPA (*dully*). I will come.

XOCHITL. You will not fail? For if you do, before tomorrow's sun I will proclaim the truth, all of it.

HUALPA. I will not fail.

(*Voices are heard within the temple.* MAXTLA *speaks, "We seek audience with the high-priestess." There is a confused murmur in answer.*)

XOCHITL. Leave me now. And do not fear. I will play my part well.

(*He nods and goes out through the garden at the right. She looks after him, then at the temple, and then she runs up the steps to the altar. Facing the well, she fastens the mask on her head, after which she flings out her arms as though in prayer. From the temple come the* THREE PRIESTESSES, *also wearing masks;* XOCHITL'S *father* MAXTLA, *and her sister* TECUICHPE. *The man is stern and dignified, his hair still black, about his shoulders an orange cape knotted on the left shoulder, and in his hair the green feather that proclaims him a cousin of the Emperor.* TECUICHPE *is a pretty, shy little thing with a fragile personality.*)

MAXTLA. We come to seek a blessing from this temple, mighty Tula. (XOCHITL *turns and bows her head, but does not speak. Her hand beckons him to come closer.*) This is my daughter, my youngest daughter, the small Tecuichpe. (TECUICHPE *kneels, her hands folded at the breast of her pale blue dress.*) Soon she weds Hualpa, the great warrior. We come to beg the soul who soon will journey to the land where dwells the mighty Mother Earth to ask her blessing on this marriage. May we remain for this secret and most awful sacrifice? (XOCHITL *nods her head, and* MAXTLA *steps back, satisfied.* TECUICHPE *stands and turns to him.*)

TECUICHPE. But, father... Hualpa should be with us, too. (XOCHITL'S *head jerks toward* TECUICHPE.)

MAXTLA (*seeing* XOCHITL'S *gesture, and thinking her displeased*). Silence, oh my daughter. I left a message for him to follow after us.

(*The* PRIESTESSES *now go up on the steps.* XOCHITL, *not being in her place, leaves a gap on one side, and there is a small excited flurry which* XOCHITL *quells.*)

XOCHITL (*her voice thickened by the mask*). Because of illness Xochitl has been sent back to her cell. Are the maidens of the city gathered before the gates?

SECOND PRIESTESS. All are there, each hoping to be the chosen one.

XOCHITL (*raising her arms*). Then we begin the sacrifice.

PRIESTESSES (*chanting*). All glory to the earth.

XOCHITL (*there grows an exultant note in her voice, as though she were defying the very gods themselves*). All glory to the Mighty Mother.

PRIESTESSES. Thus speak we, the dedicate.

XOCHITL. Keep within us the purity of wind and rain.

PRIESTESSES. Keep from us the lightning and the thunder.

XOCHITL. Keep from us the temptation of any mortal love.

PRIESTESSES. Let us remain the flowers of this garden.

XOCHITL. Let us together as a single voice adore you, Earth and Mother.

PRIESTESSES. Here forever let us stay, warm against your heart.

XOCHITL (*stepping down on the first step*). So speak we ... (*She takes a* maraca* *from the* PRIESTESS *on her left.*) ... the dedicate. (*She takes another* maraca *from the* PRIESTESS *on her right. As she crosses them triumphantly above her head,* HUALPA *hurries in from the garden.*)

TECUICHPE (*seeing him, cries out delightedly*). Hualpa, you did come in time. Poor Xochitl is ill and can not be here to add her prayer to ours for our happiness.

MAXTLA. Silence, Tecuichpe.

TECUICHPE (*draws back shyly, then, in a sudden burst of confidence, speaks to* XOCHITL). Most venerable lady, may I stand by him? He is my chosen husband, and we would pray together.

HUALPA (*terrified*). Tecuichpe! Silence!
(XOCHITL *turns her masked head toward* HUALPA, *then slowly stretches out her arm in his direction. With a gay little laugh,* TECUICHPE *runs to his side and takes his hands in hers.*)

XOCHITL (*with an undercurrent of bitter irony in her voice*). Pray. Pray now, the two of you. I want to hear you pray.

TECUICHPE (*promptly drops to her knees, then looks at* HUALPA, *who is still standing, his eyes fixed with dazed horror on* XOCHITL). Kneel. Kneel down, Hualpa.

---

* *Maraca*, a large gourd filled with shot.

Scene from AZTECA

XOCHITL: All glory to the earth. All glory to the Mighty Mother.

(HUALPA *uncertainly lifts his hand to his forehead, and then drops to one knee.*)

XOCHITL (*softly*). Pray.

TECUICHPE (*with shy dignity*). Oh, mighty Mother of Earth. Mother of all Mothers, hear my prayer. Bring to my marriage a great happiness, and the joy of sons and daughters, brave of heart and clean of limb.

XOCHITL. Have you no prayer, warrior... you who are about to wed one who loves you so well?

HUALPA (*calmly*). I have one prayer, a little one, but mighty in my heart. (*He suddenly reaches out and puts his hand on* TECUICHPE's *head.*) May sunlight form a crown about this head, and may never a single tear stain this bright face.

XOCHITL (*sharply*). Enough! Enough of prayers! You worshippers of Mighty Earth, I throw my soul into the mists of time to seek her who is most pleasant to the Earth.

PRIESTESSES (*who speak in a slow chanting tempo, and while they are speaking,* XOCHITL, *at a much faster tempo, is chanting and dancing. It is not necessary for the words of the* PRIESTESSES *to be distinct. All that is necessary is the pattern of sound*). Happy the woman chosen for this hour. Thrice happy she who goes to serve the Earth. No more of cares, no more of mortal woes. Happy the woman chosen for this hour.

XOCHITL. Hear me, oh wind and the rain. Hear me, oh thunder and lightning. Send me a sacrifice, send me a great soul, send me a soul with the feet of the hurricane, send me a soul with the power of the tempest, send me a soul to venture with courage into the mind and the heart of the earth.

(*The* PRIESTESSES *now come down from the steps and join in the dance, which has achieved a certain wild abandon.*)

PRIESTESSES (*the tempo in this passage is very fast*). Glory to the earth!

XOCHITL (*beating the* maracas). Ay-yay!

PRIESTESSES. Glory to the moon and the sun and the stars.

XOCHITL. Ay-yay! Ay-yay! Ay-yay! (*The last "ay-yay" is drawn out triumphantly.*)

PRIESTESSES. Glory to the wind!

XOCHITL. Ay-yay!

PRIESTESSES. Glory to the tree and the vine!

XOCHITL. Ay-yay! Ay-yay! Ay-yay!

PRIESTESSES. Glory to the rain!

(*The dance is growing louder and more abandoned. They are nearing the entrance to the temple.*)

XOCHITL. Ay-yay!

PRIESTESSES. Thrice glorious the rain, the husband of the earth!

XOCHITL. Ay-yay! Ay-yay! Ay-yay!
(*As she reaches the temple door,* XOCHITL *turns for one last triumphant "Ay-yay," and she sees that in watching this barbaric dance,* HUALPA *has put his arms about* TECUICHPE. *She seems to freeze where she stands, and the* PRIESTESSES *freeze with her. In a moment she walks to* TECUICHPE.)

XOCHITL. To be in love is very beautiful, but there is something more beautiful than love. The goddess has spoken. You, child, are the chosen one.

HUALPA (*horrified*). No, no, Xochitl...

XOCHITL (*smoothly*). Xochitl is ill, and can not see this last great blessing. Come, child, with me.
(*She steps backward, and as she does* TECUICHPE *moves forward, as a bird moves when charmed by a snake.*)

MAXTLA (*imploringly*). Not the only child left to me.

XOCHITL (*ignoring him*). Come to the warm arms of Mother Earth. Come to the last, the sweetest sleep of all.

TECUICHPE (*standing as though hypnotized*). How can I leave Hualpa?

XOCHITL (*beating the* maracas *in rhythm to her words*). When you leave him, you leave him free of all regrets. He will go on with no small hands to cling and blind his eyes against a greater light. Come with me to freedom, to silence, to peace.

(*During this speech she leads the girl up the steps to the altar.* MAXTLA *has lifted his cape to hide the sight from his eyes.* HUALPA *stares with horror as* TECUICHPE *lies down on the altar. As* XOCHITL *picks up the sacrificial knife and holds it triumphantly above her head, the* PRIESTESSES *begin to chant softly.*)

PRIESTESSES. Happy this soul that now will soon be free. Happy the triumph of the sacrificed, for out of pain to joy, and out of sorrow into happiness, it flies on wings of onyx and of gold into the purple cavern of the earth, where the vermilion lips of dawn are stained with the eternal gray of twilight. Oh, fortunate, most fortunate, this exultant soul.

(*As they finish their chant, the knife turns in* XOCHITL'S *hand so that the point is downward, and she smiles triumphantly down on the girl.* HUALPA *leaps forward and up on the platform.*)

XOCHITL (*screaming*). Nothing... nothing shall stop me now!

(*As the knife plunges downward,* HUALPA *reaches her, and tears the knife out of her hand.*)

PRIESTESSES (*in horror, crying out against* HUALPA). Blasphemer! Defiler of the gods!

HUALPA (*stops their concerted rush forward by pulling the mask from* XOCHITL'S *face*). No priestess this, but Xochitl, the novitiate.

XOCHITL. We are doomed. You have betrayed us both. (*She looks at the startled group.*) All of you, listen to my words. Together we have sinned against the gods. Together we have loved. Together we have sent Tula, the high-priestess, into the temple of death. This have we done, Hualpa, the warrior, and I, Xochitl, daughter of Maxtla.

(*There is a horrified silence.*)

TECUICHPE (*rising from the altar and holding out her hands*). Hualpa, tell me that this is but some terrible dream from which I soon will wake.

HUALPA. Within an hour two women have asked me the same question. Within an hour I have seen passion, death, despair. Within the tiny circle of an hour I have seen the span of life.

XOCHITL (*to the* PRIESTESSES *and* MAXTLA). Take us both to that death which awaits us. Condemn us to the black depths of the well, to any torture that your small minds can devise, for I have borne all the pain that one poor shell can feel. Come, take us both, this warrior and I.

TECUICHPE (*goes to* HUALPA). For love of me you have betrayed yourself? (*With awe.*) It was for love of me?

HUALPA. For love of you, Tecuichpe. Could I thrust back the pointed spears of Time, and with your hand in mine command the sky, then were we two in Heaven. But now I stand alone in this dark hell of my own devising, with only the white star of my love for you to lead me on to some fantastic hope.

TECUICHPE (*flings her arms about him*). Better the two of us against the whole of death, than you alone, and I to linger here.

(*Realizing her meaning,* HUALPA *laughs exultantly, and lifting her up in his arms, he jumps with her into the well.* XOCHITL *screams and runs to the edge of the well, peers down into it, then sinks down beside it, moaning.*)

PRIESTESSES (*chanting softly*). Now the wood-doves in the evening air shall call to one another two new names.

FIRST PRIESTESS. This, Xochitl, to be your punishment. Here you must linger while their souls together kneel before the topaz throne of Mother Earth.

XOCHITL (*brokenly*). Pity . . . pity for this Xochitl.

PRIESTESSES. Xochitl . . . the lonely and sad.

THE CURTAINS CLOSE

SUNDAY COSTS FIVE PESOS

A COMEDY OF MEXICAN VILLAGE LIFE

THE CHARACTERS

As originally produced by the Carolina Playmakers at Chapel Hill, North Carolina, on April 25, 1936.

FIDEL, *who is in love with Berta*	. .	Ralph Eichhorn
BERTA	. . . .	Ellen Deppe
SALOME	*friends of Berta*	Jessie Langdale
TONIA	*friends of Berta*	Christine Maynard
CELESTINA	. . . .	Jean Ashe

THE SCENE: A housed-in square in the town of the Four Cornstalks (*Las Cuatro Milpas*) in Northern Mexico.

THE TIME: The present. Early one Sunday afternoon.

THE SCENE

A housed-in square in the town called the Four Cornstalks in the northern part of Mexico. On the left of the square is the house of TONIA *with a door and a stoop. At the back is a wall cut neatly in half. The left side is the house of* BERTA, *and boasts not only a door but a barred window. On the right is a square arch from which dangles an iron lantern. This is the only exit to the rest of the town, for on the right side proper is the house of* SALOME. TONIA'S *house is pink, and* SALOME'S *is blue, while* BERTA'S *is content with being a sort of disappointed yellow. All three houses get their water from the well that is down center left.*

It is early afternoon on Sunday, and all sensible people are sleeping, but through the arch comes FIDEL DURAN. *His straw hat in his hand, his hair plastered to his head with water, he thinks he is a very handsome sight indeed as he pauses, takes a small mirror from his pocket, fixes his neck bandanna . . . a beautiful purple one with orange spots, and shyly knocks, then turns around with a broad grin on his face.*

BERTA *opens the door.* BERTA *is very pretty, but unfortunately she has a very high temper, possibly the result of her red hair. She wears a neat cotton dress and tennis shoes, blue ones. Her hands fastened on her hips, she stands and glares at* FIDEL.

BERTA. Oh, so it is you!

FIDEL (*beaming on her*). A good afternoon to you, Berta.

BERTA (*sniffing*). A good afternoon indeed, and I bothered by fools at this hour of the day.

FIDEL (*in amazement*). Why, Berta, are you angry with me?

BERTA (*questioning Heaven*). He asks me if I am angry with him. Saints in Heaven has he no memory?

FIDEL (*puzzled*). What have I done, Berta?

BERTA (*sarcastically*). Nothing, Fidel, nothing. That is the trouble. But if you come to this house again I will show you the palm of my hand, as I'm showing it to you now. (*She slaps him, steps back inside the door, and slams it shut.*)

FIDEL (*pounding on the door*). Open the door, Berta. Open the door! I must speak to you!
(*The door of* SALOME's *house opens, and* SALOME, *herself, comes out with a small pitcher and begins drawing water from the well. She is twenty-eight, and so many years of hunting a husband have left her with an acid tongue.*)

SALOME. And this is supposed to be a quiet street.

FIDEL (*who dislikes her*). You tend to your affairs, Salomé, and I will tend to mine. (*He starts pounding *again. He bleats like a young goat hunting for its mother.*) Berta, Berta.

BERTA (*opens the door again*). I will not have such noises. Do you not realize that this is Sunday afternoon? Have you no thoughts for decent people who are trying to sleep?

FIDEL. Have you no thoughts for me?

BERTA. More than one. And none of them nice.

SALOME. I would call this a lover's quarrel.

BERTA. Would you indeed! (*Glares at* FIDEL.) I would call it the impertinence of a wicked man!

FIDEL (*helplessly*). But what have I done?

SALOME. She loved him yesterday, and she will love him tomorrow.

BERTA (*runs down to* SALOME). If I love him tomorrow, may I lose the use of my tongue, yes, and my eyes and ears, too.

FIDEL (*swinging* BERTA *to one side*). Is it fair, I ask you, for a woman to smile at a man one day, and slap his face the next? Is this the manner in which a promised bride should treat her future husband?

SALOME (*grins and winks at him*). You could find yourself another bride.

BERTA (*angrily*). We do not need your advice, Salomé Molina. You and your long nose . . . sticking it in everyone's business.

SALOME (*her eyes flashing*). Is this an insult to me? To me?

BERTA. And who are you to be above insults?

SALOME. I will not stay and listen to such words!

BERTA. Did I ask you to leave the safety of your house?

SALOME (*to* FIDEL). She has not even common politeness. I am going!

BERTA. We shall adore your absence.

SALOME. If this were not Sunday, I would slap your face for you.

BERTA (*taunting*). The great Salomé Molina, afraid of a Sunday fine.

FIDEL (*wanting to be helpful*). You can fight each other tomorrow. There is no fine for week days.

SALOME. You stay out of this argument, Fidel Durán.

FIDEL. If you do not leave us I will never find out why Berta is angry with me. (*Jumps toward her.*) Go away!

SALOME (*jumps back, then tosses her head*). Very well. But the day will come when you will be glad of my company. (*She goes indignantly into her house.*)

FIDEL (*turns to* BERTA). Now, Berta.

BERTA (*interrupting*). As for you, my fine rooster, go and play the bear to Celestina García. She will appreciate you more than I.

FIDEL (*with a guilty hand to his mouth*). So that is what it is.

BERTA (*on the stoop of her own house*). That is all of it, and enough it is. Two times you walked around the plaza with the Celestina last night, and I sitting there on a bench having to watch you. (*Goes into the house.*)

FIDEL (*speaking through the open door*). But it was a matter of business.

BERTA (*enters with a broom and begins to sweep off the stoop*). Hah! Give me no such phrases. And all of my friends thinking, "Poor Berta, with such a sweetheart." Do you think I have no pride?

FIDEL. But it is that you do not understand....

BERTA. I understand enough to know that all is over between us.

FIDEL. Berta, do not say that. I love you.

BERTA. So you say. And yet you roll the eye at any passing chicken.

FIDEL. Celestina is the daughter of Don Nimfo García.

BERTA. She can be the daughter of the president for all of me. When you marry her she will bring you a fine dowry, and there will be no more need of Fidel Durán trying to carve wooden doors.

FIDEL (*his pride wounded*). Trying? But I have carved them. Did I not do a new pair for the saloon?

BERTA. Aye, little doors... doors that amount to no more than that.... (*She snaps her fingers.*) Not for you the great doors of a church.

FIDEL. Why else do you think I was speaking with the Celestina?

BERTA (*stops sweeping*). What new manner of excuse is this?

FIDEL. That is why I came to speak with you. Sit down here on the step with me for a moment.

BERTA (*scandalized*). And have Salomé and Tonia say that I am a wicked, improper girl?

FIDEL (*measuring a tiny space between his fingers*). Just for one little moment. They will see nothing.

BERTA (*sitting down*). Let the words tumble out of your mouth, one, two, three.

FIDEL. Perhaps you do not know that the town of Topo Grande, not thirty kilometers from here, is building a new church.

BERTA (*sniffs*). All the world knows that.

FIDEL. But did you know that Don Nimfo is secretly giving the money for the building of that church?

BERTA. Why?

FIDEL. He offered the money to the Blessed Virgin of Topo Grande if his rooster won in the cock-fight. It did win, so now he is building the church.

BERTA (*not yet convinced*). How did you find out about this? Or has Don Nimfo suddenly looked upon you as a son, and revealed all his secrets to you?

FIDEL. Last night on the plaza the Celestina happened to mention it. With a bit of flattery I soon gained the whole story from her.

BERTA. So that is what you were talking about as you walked around the plaza? (*Stands.*) It must have taken a great deal of flattery to gain so much knowledge from her.

FIDEL (*stands*). Do you not realize what it means? They will need someone to carve the new doors.
(*He strikes a pleased attitude, expecting her to say, "But how wonderful,* FIDEL.")

BERTA (*Knowing very well what* FIDEL *expects, promptly turns away from him, her hand hiding a smile, as she says with innocent curiosity*). I wonder whom Don Nimfo will get? (*With the delight of discovery.*) Perhaps the Brothers Ochóa from Monterrey.

FIDEL (*crestfallen*). He might choose me.

BERTA. You? Hah!

FIDEL. And why not? Am I not the best wood carver in the valley?

BERTA. So you say.

FIDEL. It would take three years to carve those doors, and he would pay me every week. There would be enough to buy you a trousseau and enough left over for a house.

BERTA. Did you tell all that to the Celestina?

FIDEL. Of course not! Does a girl help a man buy a trousseau for another girl? That was why it had to appear as though I were rolling the eye at her. (*He is very much pleased with his brilliance.*)

BERTA. Your success was more than perfect. Today all the world knows that the Celestina has won Berta's man.

FIDEL. But all the world does not know that Fidel Durán, who is I, myself, will carve those doors so as to buy a trousseau and house for Berta, my queen.

BERTA. Precisely. All the world does not know this great thing.... (*Flaring out at him.*) And neither do I!

FIDEL. Do you doubt me, pearl of my life?

BERTA. Does the rabbit doubt the snake? Does the tree doubt the lightning? Do I doubt that you are a teller of tremendous lies? Speak not to me of cleverness. I know what my own eyes see, and I saw you flirting with the Celestina. Last night I saw you . . . and so did all the world!

FIDEL (*beginning to grow angry*). So that is how you trust me, your intended husband.

BERTA. I would rather trust a hungry fox.

FIDEL. Let me speak plainly, my little dove. Because we are to be married is no reason for me to enter a monastery.

BERTA. And who says that we are to be married?

FIDEL (*taken aback*). Why . . . I said it.

BERTA. Am I a dog to your heel that I must obey your every wish?

FIDEL (*firmly*). You are my future wife.

BERTA (*laughs loudly*). Am I indeed?

FIDEL. Your mother has consented, and my father has spoken. The banns have been read in the church! (*Folds his arms with satisfaction.*)

BERTA (*screaming*). Better to die without children than to be married to such as you.

FIDEL (*screaming above her*). We shall be married within the month.

BERTA. May this hand rot on my arm if I ever sign the marriage contract.

FIDEL. Are you saying that you will not marry me?

BERTA. With all my mouth I am saying it, and a good day to you. (*Steps inside the house and slams the door. Immediately opens it and sticks her head out.*) Tell that good news to that four-nosed shrew of a Celestina. (*Slams the door again.*)

(FIDEL *puts on his hat and starts toward the archway, then runs down and pounds on* TONIA'S *door, then runs across and pounds on* SALOME'S. *In a moment both girls come out.* TONIA *is younger and smaller in size than either* SALOME *or* BERTA *and has a distressing habit of whining.*)

SALOME. What is the meaning of this noise?

TONIA. Is something wrong?

FIDEL. I call you both to witness what I say. May I drop dead if I am ever seen in this street again!

(*He settles his hat more firmly on his head, and with as much dignity as he can muster, he strides out through the arch. The girls stare after him, then at* BERTA'S *door, then at each other. Both shrug, then with one accord they run up and begin knocking on the door.*)

SALOME. Berta!

TONIA. Berta, come out!

(BERTA *enters. She is obviously trying to keep from crying.*)

SALOME. Has that fool of a sweetheart of yours lost his mind?

TONIA. What happened?

BERTA (*crying in earnest*). This day is blacker than a crow's wing. Oh, Salomé!
(*She flings both arms about the girl's neck and begins to wail loudly.* TONIA *and* SALOME *stare at each other, and then* TONIA *pats* BERTA *on the shoulder.*)

TONIA. Did you quarrel with Fidel?

SALOME. Of course she quarrelled with him. Any fool could see that.

BERTA. He will never come back to me. Never!

TONIA (*to* SALOME). Did she say anything about the Celestina to him?

SALOME (*to* BERTA). You should have kept your mouth shut on the outside of your teeth.

BERTA. A girl has her pride, and no Celestina is going to take any man of mine.

TONIA. But did she take him?

BERTA (*angrily to* TONIA). You take your face away from here!

SALOME. The only thing you can do now is to ask him to come back to you.

TONIA (*starting toward the archway*). I will go and get him.

BERTA (*clutches at her*). I will wither on my legs before I ask him to come back. He would never let me forget that I had to beg him to marry me. (*Wails again.*) And now he will marry the Celestina. (TONIA *begins to cry with her.*)

TONIA. There are other men.

BERTA. My heart is with Fidel. My life is ruined.

SALOME (*thoughtfully*). If we could bring him back without his knowing Berta had sent for him.... (*She sits on the edge of the well.*)

TONIA. Miracles only happen in the church.

SALOME (*catches her knee and begins to rock back and forth*). What could we tell him? What could we tell him?

TONIA. You be careful, Salomé, or you will fall in the well. Then we will all have to go into mourning, and Berta cannot get married at all if she is in mourning.

SALOME (*snaps her fingers*). You could fall down the well, Berta! That would bring him back.

BERTA (*firmly*). I will not fall down the well and drown for any man, not even Fidel.

TONIA. What good would bringing him back do if Berta were dead?

SALOME. Now that is a difficulty. (*Begins to pace up and down.*) If you are dead, you cannot marry Fidel. If you are not dead, he will not come back. The only thing left for you is to die an old maid.

TONIA. That would be terrible.

BERTA (*wailing*). My life is ruined. Completely ruined.

SALOME (*with sudden determination*). Why? Why should it be?

TONIA (*with awe*). Salomé has had a thought.

BERTA. You do not know what a terrible thing it is to lose the man you love.

SALOME. I am fixing up your life, not mine. Suppose... suppose you did fall in the well.

BERTA. I tell you I will not do it.

SALOME. Not really, but suppose he thought you did. What then?

BERTA. You mean . . . pretend? But that is a sin! The priest would give me ten days' penance at confessional.

SALOME (*flinging out her hands*). Ten days' penance or a life without a husband. Which do you choose?

TONIA. I will tell you. She chooses the husband. What do we do, Salomé?

SALOME. You run and find this carver of doors. Tell him that a great scandal has happened . . . that Berta has fallen in the well.

TONIA (*whose dramatic imagination has begun to work*). Because she could not live without him. . . .

BERTA. You tell him that and I will scratch out both your eyes!

TONIA. On Sunday?

BERTA (*sullenly*). On any day.

SALOME. Tell him that Berta has fallen in the well, and that you think she is dying.

TONIA. Is that all?

BERTA. Is that not enough?

SALOME (*entranced with the idea*). Oh, it will be a great scene, with Berta so pale in her bed, and Fidel kneeling in tears beside it.

BERTA. I want you to know that I am a modest girl.

SALOME (*irritated*). You can lie down on the floor then. (*Glaring at* TONIA.) What are you standing there for? Run!

TONIA (*starts toward the archway, then comes back*). But . . . where will I go?

SALOME. To the place where all men go with a broken heart . . . the saloon. Are you going to stand there all day?

(TONIA *gives a little gasp and runs out through the arch.*)

BERTA. I do not like this idea. If Fidel finds out it is a trick, he will be angrier than ever.

SALOME. But if he does not find out the truth until after you are married . . . what difference will it make?

BERTA. He might beat me.

SALOME. Leave that worry until after you are married. (*Inspecting* BERTA.) Now how will we make you look pale? Have you any flour? Corn meal might do.

BERTA. No! No! I will not do it.

SALOME. Now, Berta, be reasonable.

BERTA. If I had really fallen down the well, it would be different. But I did not fall down it.

SALOME. Do you not want Fidel to come back to you? Are you in love with him?

BERTA. Yes, I do love him. And I will play no tricks on him. If he loves the Celestina better than he does me... (*with great generosity*) He can marry her.

SALOME (*pleading with such idiocy*). But Tonia has gone down to get him. If he comes back and finds you alive... he will be angrier than ever.

BERTA (*firmly*). This is your idea. You can get out of it the best way you can. But Fidel will not see me lying down on a bed, nor on a floor, nor any place else.

SALOME. Then there is only one thing to do.

BERTA. What is that?

SALOME. You will go into the house, and I will tell him that you are too sick to see him.

BERTA. That will be just as bad as the other.

SALOME. How can it be? Then if he finds out it is a trick, he will blame me, and you can pretend you knew nothing of it. I do not care how angry he is. I do not want to marry him.

BERTA (*with pleased excitement*). Then he could not be angry with me, could he? I mean if he thought I had nothing to do with it? And I would not have to do penance either, would I?

SALOME. Not one day of penance. Tonia should have found him by now. (*Goes to the arch and peers through.*) Here they come . . . and Fidel is running half a block in front of her.

BERTA (*joyously*). Then he does love me!

SALOME. Into the house with you. You can watch through the window.

BERTA (*on stoop*). Now, remember, if he gets angry, this was your idea.

SALOME (*claps her hands*). And what a beautiful idea it is! (BERTA *disappears into the house.* SALOME *looks about her, then dashes over to her own stoop, sits down, flings her shawl over her face, and begins to moan loudly, rocking back and forth. In a moment* FIDEL *dashes through the arch, and stops, out of breath, at seeing* SALOME.)

FIDEL (*gasping*). Berta!

SALOME (*whose moaning grows louder*). Poor darling, poor darling. She was so young.

FIDEL (*desperately*). She is . . . she is dead?

SALOME (*wailing*). She will make such a beautiful corpse. Poor darling. Poor darling.
(TONIA *exhausted and out of breath, has reached the arch.*)

TONIA (*looks about her in astonishment*). Why, where is Berta? Did she go into the house?

SALOME (*in normal tones*). Of course she went into the house, you fool. Did she not jump down the well? (*Remembering* FIDEL.) Poor darling.

TONIA (*blankly*). Did she really jump down it? I thought she just fell in by accident.

SALOME (*grimly*). Are you telling this story... or am I? (*Wailing.*) Now she can never go to the plaza again.

(FIDEL *looks helplessly from* TONIA, *who cannot quite get the details of the story straight, to* SALOME *who is having a beautiful time mourning.*)

FIDEL. Where is she? I want to see her.

TONIA (*coming out of her trance*). She is right in here. Did you say she was on the bed or on the floor, Salomé?

SALOME (*getting between them and* BERTA's *door*). You don't want to see her, Fidel. You know how people look after they've been drowned.

TONIA. But he was supposed to see her. That was why you sen...

SALOME (*glaring at her*). Tonia, dear, suppose that you let me tell the story. After all, I was here and you were not.

FIDEL (*exploding*). For the love of the saints, tell me! Is she dead?

SALOME (*thinking this over*). Well... not exactly.

FIDEL. You mean... you mean there is hope?

SALOME. I would say there was great hope.

FIDEL (*takes off his hat and mops his face*). What can I do? Oh, if I could only see her....

SALOME. If you would go to the church and light a candle to Our Blessed Lady and ask her to forgive you for getting angry with Berta... perhaps things will arrange themselves.

FIDEL. Do you think she will get well soon?

SALOME. With a speed that will amaze you.

FIDEL. I will go down and light the candle right now. (*As he turns to leave, who should come through the archway but* CELESTINA GARCIA. *She can match temper for temper with* BERTA *any day, and right now she is on the war-path. Brushing past these three as though they did not exist, she goes up to* BERTA'S *door and pounds on it.*)

CELESTINA. I dare you to come out and call this Celestina García a four-nosed shrew to her face.

SALOME (*trying to push* FIDEL *through the arch*). You had best run to the church.

FIDEL (*pushing past her and going up to* CELESTINA). How dare you speak like that to a poor drowned soul?

SALOME (*to Celestina*). Why do you not go away? We never needed you so little.

CELESTINA. So she is pretending to be drowned, eh? Is that her coward's excuse?

BERTA (*through window*). Who dares to call Berta Cantú a coward?

CELESTINA. You know well enough who calls you, and I the daughter of Don Nimfo García.

TONIA. Ai, Salomé! And now Fidel will know that Berta was not drowned at all.

FIDEL (*who has been listening to this conversation with growing surprise and suspicion, now turns furiously toward* BERTA'S *house*). Not drowned, eh? So this was a trick to bring me back, eh? I am through with your tricks, you hear me? Through with them!

BERTA (*through window*). You stay right there until I come out. (*She disappears from view.*)

FIDEL (*turning to* SALOME). I see your hand in this.

SALOME. The more fool you to be taken in by a woman's tricks.

CELESTINA. What care I for tricks? No woman is going to call me names!

BERTA (*coming through the door*). You keep silence, Celestina García. I will deal with you in a minute. And as for you, Fidel Durán....

FIDEL (*stormily*). As for me, I am finished with all women. The world will see me no more. I will enter a monastery and carve as many doors as I like. Do you hear me, Berta Cantú?

BERTA (*putting both hands over her ears*). What do I care for your quack, quack, quack!

FIDEL. Now she calls me a duck! Good afternoon to you! (*He stalks out with wounded dignity.*)

CELESTINA (*catching* BERTA *by the shoulder and swinging her around*). I ask you again; Did you call me a four-nosed shrew?

BERTA. I did, and I will repeat it with the greatest of pleasure. You are a four-nosed shrew and a three-eyed frog!

CELESTINA. I have always looked on you as my friend... you pink-toed cat!

BERTA. And I have always trusted you... you sly robber of bridegrooms!
(*She raises her hand to slap* CELESTINA. SALOME *catches it.*)

SALOME. This is Sunday, Berta! And Sunday costs five pesos.

TONIA. If you had to pay a fine for starting a fight on top of losing Fidel.... Ay, that would be terrible.

(BERTA *and* CELESTINA *glare at each other, and then slowly begin to circle each other, spitting out their insults as they do so.*)

CELESTINA. It is my honor that is making me fight, or I would wait until tomorrow.

BERTA. If I had five pesos to throw away, I would pull out your dangling tongue... leaving only the flapping roots.

CELESTINA. Ha! I make a nose at your words.

BERTA. As for you...you eater of ugly smelling cheese....

(*They jump at each other, but remember the penalty just in time and pull back. Again they begin to circle around, contenting themselves with making faces at each other.* SALOME *suddenly clasps her hands.*)

SALOME. You are both certain that you want to fight today?

CELESTINA. Why else do you think I came here?

BERTA. These insults have gone too far to stop now.

SALOME. The only thing that stands in the way is the five pesos for the Sunday fine.

TONIA. And five pesos is a lot of money.

SALOME. Then the only thing to do is to play the fingers.

CELESTINA. What?

BERTA. Eh?

SALOME. Precisely. Whoever loses strikes the first blow and pays the fine. Then you can fight as much as you like.

TONIA (*with awed admiration*). Ay, Salomé, you have so many brains.

CELESTINA (*doubtfully*). It is a big risk.

BERTA (*shrugging*). Perhaps you are afraid of taking a risk.

CELESTINA. I am not afraid of anything. But Tonia will have to be the judge. Salomé is too clever.

BERTA. Very well. But Salomé has to stand behind you to see that you do not cheat. I would not trust you any more than I would a mouse near a piece of fresh bacon.

CELESTINA (*pulls back her clenched fist, then thinks better of it, and speaks with poor grace*). Very well. (CELESTINA *and* BERTA *stand facing each other.* TONIA *stands between them up on the stoop.* SALOME *stands behind* CELESTINA.)

TONIA (*feeling a little nervous over this great honor of judging*). Both arms behind your backs. (*The girls link their arms behind them.*) Now, when I drop my hand, Berta will guess first as Celestina brings her fingers forward. The first girl to guess correctly twice wins. Are you ready? (*All nod.*) I am going to drop my arm.

SALOME. Celestina, put out your fingers before Berta guesses. We will have no cheating.

CELESTINA (*sullenly*). Very well. (*She puts out two fingers behind her, and* SALOME, *seeing this, raises up her arm with two fingers extended, opening and closing them scissors fashion.* BERTA *frowns a little as she looks up at the signal and* CELESTINA, *seeing this, swings around and looks at* SALOME, *who promptly grins warmly and pretends to be waving at* BERTA. CELESTINA *then looks at* TONIA.)

BERTA. Very well.

CELESTINA (*guessing as* BERTA *swings her arm forward*). Three.

(BERTA *triumphantly holds up one finger. Biting her lip,* CELESTINA *starts to swing forward her own arm.* SALOME, *intent on signalling* BERTA, *holds up her own five fingers spread wide, and does not notice until too late that* CELESTINA *has swung around to watch her.*)

CELESTINA (*screaming*). So I cheat, eh? (*With that she gives* SALOME *a resounding slap on the cheek. The next moment the two women are mixed up in a beautiful howling, grunting fight, while* TONIA *and* BERTA, *wide-eyed, cling together and give the two women as much space as possible. Let it be understood that this is only a*

Scene from SUNDAY COSTS FIVE PESOS

TONIA: I was on the bottom once, and I won!

fight of kicking, hair-pulling and scratching. There is no man involved, nor a point of honor. Rather a matter of angry pride. So the two are not attempting to mutilate each other. They are simply gaining satisfaction. The grand finale comes when CELESTINA knocks SALOME *to the ground and sits on her.*)

CELESTINA (*breathing hard*). There! That was worth five pesos.

TONIA. You have to pay it. And Don Nimfo will be angry with you.

CELESTINA (*pulling herself to her feet*). I am too tired to fight any more now, but I will be back next Tuesday, Berta, and then I will beat you up.

BERTA (*sniffing*). If you can.

CELESTINA (*warningly*). And there is no fine on Tuesday.

BERTA. Come any day you like. I will be ready for you.

TONIA (*to* CELESTINA). You should be ashamed to fight.

CELESTINA. Who are you to talk to me? (*Stamps her foot at* TONIA *who jumps behind* BERTA.) Good afternoon my brave little rabbits!

(*She staggers out as straight as she can, but as she reaches the archway she feels a twinge of agony and is forced to limp. By this time* SALOME *has gathered together what strength she has left, and she slowly stands up. Once erect, she looks at* Berta *and* Tonia *as though she were considering boiling in oil too good for them.*)

Salome (*with repressed fury*). My friends. My very good friends.

Tonia (*frightened*). Now, Salomé....

Salome (*screaming*). Do not speak to me! Either of you! (*She manages to get to the door of her house.*) When I need help, do you give me aid? No! But just you wait... both of you!

Tonia. What are you going to do?

Salome. I am going to wait for a week-day, and then I am going to beat up both of you at once. One (*she takes a deep breath*) with each hand! (*She nearly falls through the door of her house.*)

Berta (*with false bravado*). Who is afraid of her?

Tonia. I am. Salomé is very strong. It is all your fault. If you had not gotten mad at Fidel, this would not have happened.

Berta (*snapping at her*). You leave Fidel out of this.

Tonia (*beginning to cry*). When Salomé beats me up, that will be your fault too.

Berta. Stop crying!

TONIA. I am not a good fighter, but I can tell Fidel the truth about how you would not jump down the well to win him back.

BERTA. You open your mouth to Fidel and I will push you in the well.

TONIA. You will not have strength enough to push a baby in the well when they get through with you.

BERTA. Get out! Get out of here! (*She stamps her foot at* TONIA *and the girl, frightened, gives a squeak and runs into her own house.* BERTA *looks after her, then, beginning to sniffle, she goes over and sits on the well. She acts like a child who has been told that it is not proper for little girls to cry, and she is very much in need of a handkerchief. Just then* FIDEL *sticks his head around the arch.*)

FIDEL (*once more the plaintive goat*). Berta.
(BERTA *half jumps, then pretends not to hear him.*)

FIDEL (*enters cautiously, not taking his eyes off of* BERTA'S *stiff back. He moves around at the back, skirts* TONIA'S *house, then works his way round to her*). Berta.

BERTA (*sniffling*). What is it?

FIDEL (*circling the back of the well*). Are you crying, Berta?

BERTA (*stubbornly*). No!

FIDEL (*sitting beside her*). Yes, you are. I can see you crying.

BERTA. If you can see, why do you ask, then?

FIDEL. I am sorry we quarrelled, Berta.

BERTA. Are you?

FIDEL. Are you sorry?

BERTA. No!

FIDEL. I was hoping you were, because... do you know whom I saw on the plaza?

BERTA. Grandfather Devil.

FIDEL. Don Nimfo himself.

BERTA. Perhaps you saw the Celestina, too.

FIDEL (*placatingly*). Now, Berta, you know I do not care if I never see the Celestina again. (*Pulls out a handkerchief and extends it to her.*) Here, wipe your face with this.

BERTA. I have a handkerchief of my own. (*Nevertheless she takes it, and wipes her eyes and then blows her nose.*)

FIDEL. Don Nimfo said I could carve the church doors for him. But he said I would have to move to Topo

Grande to work on them. He said I had to leave right away.

BERTA (*perking up her interest*). You mean... move away from here?

FIDEL. And I was wondering if we could get married tomorrow. I know this is very sudden, Berta, but after all, think how long I have waited to carve a church door.

BERTA. Tomorrow. (*She looks toward* SALOME's *house.*) They would both be too sore to do anything by tomorrow.

FIDEL (*too concerned with his own plans to hear what she is saying*). Of course I know that you may not be able to forgive me....

BERTA. Fidel, I want you to understand that if I do marry you tomorrow... that means we will leave here tomorrow, eh?

FIDEL. Ay, yes. I have to be in Topo Grande on Tuesday.

BERTA. I hope you will always understand what a great thing I have done for you. It is not every girl who would forgive so easily as I.

FIDEL (*humbly*). Indeed, I know that, Berta.

BERTA. Are you quite sure that we will leave here tomorrow?

FIDEL. Quite sure.

BERTA. Very well. I will marry you.

FIDEL (*joyfully*). Berta! (*Bends forward to kiss her. She jumps up.*)

BERTA. Just a moment. We are not married yet. Do you think that I am just any girl that you can kiss me... like that! (*She snaps her fingers.*)

FIDEL (*humbly*). I thought... just this once....

BERTA (*gravely thoughtful*). Well, perhaps... just this once... you may kiss my hand.

As he kisses it

THE CURTAINS CLOSE

APPENDICES

ON MEXICAN COSTUME

GENERAL

There are two general conceptions in the United States of the Mexican woman's costume:

1. That she wears a high comb, a lace shawl draped over it, a ruffled skirt, a rose in her mouth and a dagger in her garter.

2. That she wears a glittering, bespangled red and green skirt, a white blouse, a rose in her hair and a dagger in her garter.

Both of these images are, needless to say, romantic dreams. As a friend of mine once said, a Mexican girl wears her daggers in her eyes, her roses in her lips and cheeks, and her glittering spangles in her personality, which, I think, is very close to the truth.

The costume indicated under (1) above is purely Spanish, and disappeared from Mexico after the Revolution of 1810 when the Republic ceased to be a colony of Spain. The (2) costume can be seen in Mexico on the stage, and amongst the common people on feast days. As the skirts seldom weigh under twenty-five pounds, they are not exactly practical for everyday use.

This does not mean that the Mexican women of the lower classes, with whom my plays deal, do not wear color. They do. They glory in it. But their skirts are made of muslin or some other cheap material. The most common color is a brilliant, unashamed pink, closely followed in popularity by bright red, lilac, blue, and green. Often the skirts are striped in two colors, such as blue and white, pink and white, or blue and pink.

The blouses are sometimes white, but more often colored, a popular combination being a red blouse with a pink skirt, or an orange blouse with a green or blue skirt. By some magic sucked from nature, regardless of the combination of colors she puts on, a Mexican woman is never garish.

She rarely uses shoes, preferring the feel of the earth under her feet, although she may condescend to leather sandals, brightly colored tennis shoes, or black oxfords. Once in a while she will wear rope-soled sandals called *alpargatas,* which are of Basque origin. I can't remember ever having seen a lower-class Mexican woman with white shoes on her feet.

She loves beads, bracelets, and rings of the ten cent store variety. Immediately after she is born her ears are punctured for earrings, because of the belief that puncturing the ears improves and preserves the eyesight. These rings are invariably of pure gold, and most of them are very old and beautiful.

Her hair is her chief glory. Whether blonde, brunette, or red-head, it is carefully brushed and oiled every day until it shines, and is washed in rain water and soap root, which keeps it soft and pliable. As a general rule it is parted in the center and worn in two heavy plaits that fall forward over the shoulders. As civilization creeps onward into the villages, however, this mode is fast dying out in favor of hair cut in a long bob. Regardless of how she wears it, right at the back of the crown will be thrust a low semicircular comb of bright red, pink, green, or white celluloid. A girl such as CRICKET in *Soldadera* would wear seven or eight of these combs thrust into the sides and back of the hair. Nice girls never wear more than three: one in the back and one on each side. Even the older women, who are always dressed entirely in black, wear them, although they forego all other jewelry save their wedding-rings, their earrings, and their holy medals worn on a string around the neck.

The older women are inveterate smokers, preferring corn-husk cigarettes, which extinguish as easily as a corn-cob pipe. When not in use these are thrust for safe-keeping above the right ear in the same manner that a man carries a pencil.

In cold weather all lower-class women wear a large square wool shawl, generally a light blue, worn with a triangle fold. A widow uses a square black voile shawl without fringe, which, when held up, is as long as she is tall. One side of this is put around the head nun-fashion, and fastened under the chin with a black safety-pin. The rest of it is allowed to hang free in the manner of a long cape. On Sundays a small triangle or square of thin black lace is used for church services. This is allowed to rest lightly on the hair and is probably the most beautiful frame for a woman's face that was ever invented.

There is one more shawl, however, without which no lower-class woman would be seen in public. Regardless of the heat or the cold, of whether she is in the house or out of it, she would as soon be seen without her clothes as without her *rebozo*. This is the national shawl of Mexico, and is almost impossible to describe, since it is used in no other country. I have seen them woven of the finest silk, at least twelve feet in length, and so pliable that they can be drawn through a baby's ring. Others, of a heavier weave, are as short as six feet in length. I have never seen one shorter than that, save for the use of children. As a general rule they are three feet wide, although some are six feet wide and are worn doubled. No fringe is added to the sides, but the thread from which the shawl is woven is knotted into fringe hanging about a foot deep on both ends. In color, save for the feast day costume of which it is as integral a part as the sequins and embroidery, it is dark in tone, being blue, green, or, most popularly, a very dark red.

It is useful as well as ornamental. It serves as combination hat and raincoat by being draped over the head and shoulders and around the forearms. Knotted around the throat it makes an excellent sling in which to carry a baby on the back. One end of it rolled in a flat circle and placed on the head makes an excellent support for a pail, a basket, or a wooden washboard, thus leaving the arms free for other bundles. When worn across the head, one end of it is draped half across the face—across the nose and mouth by older women to prevent "catching the air"—a dreaded Mexican sickness; or across one eye and the lower part of the face by a young girl, as this makes the visible eye extremely provocative to any passing man. As the Indians of Mexico do not use veils, this is doubtless a relic of the Moors' conquest of Spain.

Regardless of how she uses it, the Mexican woman *always* uses it, combined with any other veils she may also be wearing. In the south of the Republic, where hats are used as a protection against the sun, men's straw sombreros are often seen perched on top of a *rebozo* draped over the head. The constant use of this shawl, prevalent all over the Republic (although each state has its own method of draping it) is one of the minor mysteries of Mexico that will probably never be solved. They are not cheap, and many a poor woman has had to do without food in order to buy one. However, there is never any sense of rivalry over them, such as "My shawl is better or more beautiful than yours."

The men, like the women, love color. In the north, where the trousers are generally of American make, the shirts are always colored, and preferably silk. A storekeeper told me that in thirty years of business he has never sold a white shirt. These shirts are pink, lavender, yellow, tan, and orange in that order of preference. In the summer white duck trousers are popular. In the winter a plain gray, dark brown, or white blanket is worn with a hole slit in the middle through which the head is passed. This serves as an overcoat in the daytime and a cover at night. The hat is a straw sombrero with a high peaked crown, or a stiff-brimmed Texas hat, relic of the days of Villa.

The lower-class man wears leather sandals or *alpargatas*, the latter generally if he is quite old. For feast days he wears bright yellow buttoned shoes with a puffed toe. He rarely if ever wears socks. He always wears a brightly figured bandanna knotted about his throat, never about his head. His only jewelry is his wedding-ring and a holy medal strung on a cord about his neck. His ears are never pierced for earrings because, being a man and superior, his eyesight is naturally better than a woman's.

The farther south one travels, the more the man's costume changes. His trousers are made of *manta*, which closely resembles unbleached domestic. Sometimes the legs are folded over so as to fit closely at the ankles. Sometimes they are folded over to end at the shin. In Michoacan one leg hangs loosely to the ankle, the other is folded up to the knee. In Vera Cruz the trousers are very wide and are worn with a brilliant purple shirt.

The hat also changes. Near Mexico City, the crown stays high, but the brim is decidedly large with a high upward roll. In Michoacan the brim is large, but the crown is low and flat. In Vera Cruz panamas are worn.

Regardless of the state, the bandanna, like the woman's *rebozo*, is an essential part of the costume. In some states a brilliantly colored apron shaped like a triangle is worn open on one hip and knotted on the other. In many states a short blanket, ending at the hips, is worn, a slit in the center permitting it to pass over the head. This may be either oblong or triangular in shape, and is always brilliantly colored. Sometimes a long, plain colored blanket is worn folded and slung over one shoulder.

These costume notes refer, of course, to the lower classes, with which my plays deal. It would need a full-sized volume to classify completely the costumes of Mexico, many of which are indigenous to their own particular state.

As for make-up, the lower-class Mexicans of my plays do not have the copper-colored skin of the American Indians, nor are they the rusty-brown of the Texas Mexican. Rather they resemble the average well-tanned American. The cheek-bones are high; the skeleton structure of the women small and delicate regardless of their plumpness; the men are muscular and on the average stocky, although the northern Mexican man is quite often large both as to size and weight.

The theory that all Mexicans are brunettes is untrue. Many Mexicans are quite blond, with yellow hair and green eyes; and dark red hair with freckles is common coloring.

Like the United States, Mexico is a melting pot of all nations, Irish, German and Spanish being the three most popular foreign strains. However, I have yet to meet a man with possibly no more than a single drop of Indian blood, who does not say proudly, "I am a true Mexican."

AZTECAN

The Aztecans, although a cultured race, possessed enough barbaric traits to love brilliant colors and many ornaments. When gathered before their temples they looked like a field of flaming tropical flowers.

For purposes of religious mystery the priests wore masks, the fine lacquer ones being anywhere from six inches to three feet larger than their normal faces. These giant masks were mostly caricatures of the human face, the lips lengthened, the forehead wrinkled, the nose curved so as to give the impression of demons. It is such masks as these that the priestesses wear in *Azteca.* The *Encyclopædia Britannica* gives instructions for making them from papier-maché. For purposes of production it is suggested that Xochitl's mask be solid black. The older priestesses should wear masks with a brilliant color base over which are splashed other colors.

For headdresses, pieces of supple, white cardboard, twisted into a very high crown and painted with barbaric designs will serve.

In clothing it must be remembered that the Aztecan woman of rank was extremely modest. Sandals covered the bare feet. A long skirt ended at the ankles, over which was worn a straight, unbelted tunic which fell from the shoulders, and was embroidered in flashing colors. A square- or V-neck, not cut too low, was worn, and butterfly sleeves ending at the top of the arm, while wide, gold bracelets were clasped above and below the elbows.

HUALPA wears close-fitting, vividly-stenciled cloth hose ending at the ankles. Over these a short doublet, also stenciled, with a high round neck, close sleeves ending just above the elbow, and the doublet itself falling almost to the knees. These doublets were cut princess style with the skirt cut just wide enough to provide easy movement. He, too, wears bracelets, and around his neck a chain from which dangles a large round medallion. At his back a flint knife is strapped. His black hair, falling straight about the cheeks, is banged across the forehead.

MAXTLA wears a long tunic ending about three inches above the ankle. Sleeves and neck are like HUALPA's. A square cape, almost as long as his tunic, is worn under the right arm, tying in a large rabbit-knot on the left shoulder. His costume is also brilliantly stenciled.

Maracas are large gourds filled with shot. They may be procured from any music store.

ON SPANISH PRONUNCIATION

Of all the Latin languages, Spanish is doubtless the easiest for the foreigner to pronounce. Being a phonetic language, every syllable is given its full value, and all end vowels are sounded.

The alphabet, which differs very slightly from the English, is the following, with the sound of the letter as heard in English beside it, not the actual name of the letter in Spanish:

a: as in mama
b: as the *v* in vicar
c: as in cap
ch: as in chew
d: as the *th* in the
e: as the *a* in day
f: as in fantasy
g: as in gay
h: is a silent letter. The syllable carries the sound of the vowel immediately following the *h*. *Example:* Hi-lar-io is pronounced as though it were written i-lar-io.
i: as the *e* in me
j: as the *h* in have
k: rarely used. Carries the sound of *c* in cap.
l: as in lamp
ll: In Mexico this *always* carries the sound of *y* in yellow.
m: as in more

n: as in no
ñ: as the *ny* in canyon. Thus doña is pronounced don-ya.
o: as in over
p: as in paper
q: Generally governed by the vowel that follows it. The safest rule is to sound it as the *c* in car.
r: pronounced softly as in route.
rr: a harsher *r*. Sounds like a Scotchman saying "red."
s: as in sold
t: as in tempest
u: as the double *o* in moon
v: as in vowel
w: this letter does not exist in the Spanish alphabet
x: as a general rule carries the sound of *h* in have
y: at the beginning of a syllable carries the sound of *y* in yellow. When standing alone it has the sound of *e* in me. *Example:* Martinez y Lopez.
z: a sharp *s* as in suspect. In Mexico it is never pronounced *th*.
ua: the most commonly used diphthong in Spanish is pronounced *wa* as in water.

The rules of accentuation are easy and simple to follow. Excepting in the case of an accent appearing above a syllable, as, for example, capitán, the following two rules invariably apply:

1. All words ending in a consonant, excepting *n* or *s*, are accented on the last syllable.
   Example: Fi-*del*.
2. All words ending in a vowel, and *n* or *s*, are accented on the next to the last syllable.
   Example: Jua-*ni*-ta, An-*sel*-mo, *Ber*-ta. (To-*más*, al-

though ending in an *s*, carries a written accent above the *a*, which throws the stress to that syllable. The same applies to Sal-o-*mé*.)

The combination *ia* generally carries a written accent above the *i*, meaning that the *i*, forming a syllable with the consonant immediately preceding it, is to be stressed. *Example:* Ma-*rí*-a.

www.ingramcontent.com/pod-product-compliance
Lightning Source LLC
LaVergne TN
LVHW041928090826
845145LV00017B/2034

* 9 7 8 1 4 6 9 6 4 0 2 8 0 *